THE SATURDAY EVENING POST

Saga of The American West

THE SATURDAY EVENING POST

Saga of The American West

the land, the lives, the legacy

THE CURTIS PUBLISHING COMPANY
Indianapolis, Indiana

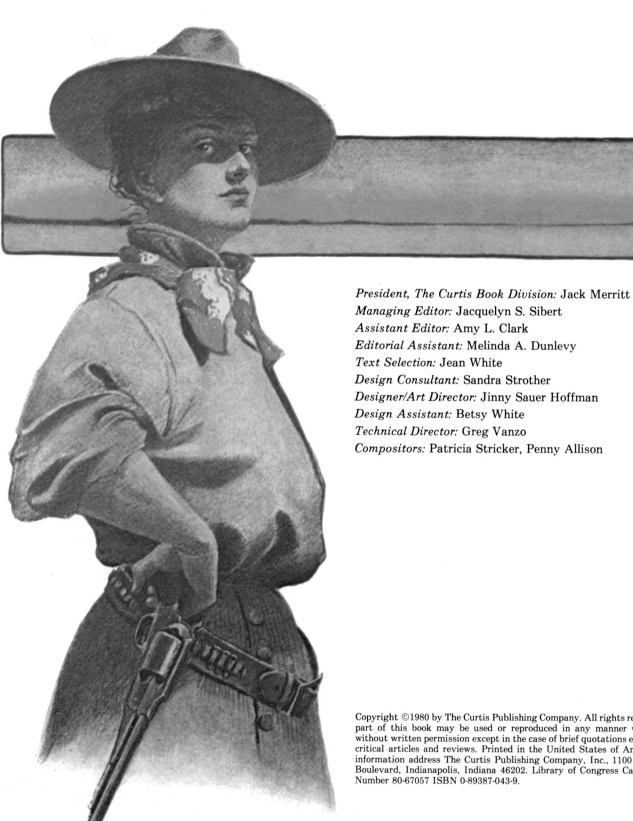

President, The Curtis Book Division: Jack Merritt
Managing Editor: Jacquelyn S. Sibert
Assistant Editor: Amy L. Clark
Editorial Assistant: Melinda A. Dunlevy
Text Selection: Jean White
Design Consultant: Sandra Strother
Designer/Art Director: Jinny Sauer Hoffman
Design Assistant: Betsy White
Technical Director: Greg Vanzo
Compositors: Patricia Stricker, Penny Allison

Contents

The *Tourist* and the *Tenderfoot*

The West Held
Their Fortune

Old Times in San Francisco

Reminiscences by **Bret Harte**

Few writers are more closely identified with a geographical area than Bret Harte with California. Harte was born in Albany, New York, but he was just 18 when, after his father's death and his mother's remarriage, he arrived in San Francisco. The year was 1854. Harte was in his sixties and living quietly in London when he wrote this description of the lively city by the bay as he first knew it, for a 1900 issue of the Post.

One of my recollections is of "steamer night," as it was called—the night of "steamer day"—preceding the departure of the mail steamship for "home." Indeed, at that time San Francisco may be said to have lived from steamer day to steamer day; bills were made due on that day, interest computed to that period and accounts settled. The next day was the turning of a new leaf, another assay to fortune, another inspiration of energy. So recognized was the fact that even ordinary changes of condition, social and domestic, were put aside until *after* steamer day. "I'll see what I can do after next steamer day" was the common cautious or hopeful formula. It was the "Saturday night" of many a wage-earner—and to him a night of festivity. The thoroughfares were animated and crowded; the saloons and theaters full. I can recall at such times wandering along the City Front, as the business part of San Francisco was then known. Here the lights were burning

all night, the first streaks of dawn finding the merchants still at their counting-house desks. I remember the dim lines of warehouses lining the insecure wharves of rotten piles, half filled in—that had ceased to be wharves but had not yet become streets—their treacherous yawning depths, with the uncertain gleam of tarlike mud below, at times still vocal with the lap and gurgle of the tide. I remember the weird stories of disappearing men found afterward imbedded in the ooze in which they had fallen and gasped their life away. I remember the two or three ships, still left standing where they were beached a year or two before, built in between warehouses, their bows projecting into the roadway. There was the dignity of the sea and its boundless freedom in their beautiful curves which the abutting houses could not destroy, and even something of the sea's loneliness in the far-spaced ports and cabin windows lit up by the lamps of the prosaic landsmen who plied their trades behind them. One of these ships, transformed into a hotel, retained its name, the *Niantic,* and part of its characteristic interior remained unchanged. I remember these ships' old tenants—the rats—who had increased to such an extent that at night they fearlessly crossed the wayfarer's path at every turn, the gilded saloons of and even invaded In the *Niantic* their Montgomery Street. on every pitapat was met staircase, and it was said that sometimes

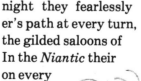

"Steamer day," for trade no longer depended upon the trade winds, launched its observers once again after fortune.

in an excess of sociability they accompanied the traveler to his room. In the early "cloth-and-papered" houses—so called because the ceilings were not plastered, but simply covered by stretched and white-washed cloth—their scamperings were plainly indicated in zigzag movements of the sagging cloth, or they became actually visible by finally dropping through the holes they had worn in it! I remember the house whose foundations were made of boxes of plug tobacco, part of a jettisoned cargo used instead of more expensive lumber; and the adjacent warehouse where the trunks of the early and forgotten forty-niners were stored, and—never claimed by their dead or missing owners—were finally sold at auction. I remember the strong breath of the sea over all and the constant onset of the trade winds which helped to disinfect the

deposits of dirt and grime, decay and wreckage which were stirred up in the later evolutions of the city.

Or I recall, with the same sense of youthful satisfaction and unabated wonder, my wanderings through the Spanish Quarter, where three centuries of quaint customs, speech and dress were still preserved; where the proverbs of Sancho Panza were still spoken in the language of Cervantes, and the high-flown illusions of the La Manchian knights still a part of the Spanish Californian hidalgo's dream. I recall the more modern Mexican—his index finger steeped in cigarette stains; his velvet jacket and his crimson sash; the many-flounced skirts and lace manta of his women, and their caressing intonations—the one musical utterance of the whole hard-voiced city.

Perhaps from my Puritan training I experienced a

fearful joy in the gambling saloons. They were the largest and most comfortable, even as they were the most expensively decorated rooms in San Francisco. Here, gravity and decorum were present. People staked and lost their last dollar with calm solemnity and resignation. The oaths, exclamations and feverish interruptions which often characterized more dignified assemblies were absent here. There was no room for the lesser vices; there was little or no drunkenness; the gaudily dressed and painted women who presided over the wheels of fortune or performed on the harp and piano- attracted no attention from those ascetic players. The man who had won ten thousand dollars and the man who had lost everything rose from the table with equal silence and imperturbability. *I* never witnessed any tragic sequel to those losses; *I* never heard of any suicide on account of them. Neither can I recall any quarrel or murder directly attributable to this kind of gambling. It must be remembered that these public games were chiefly *rouge et noir*, monte, faro, or roulette, in which the antagonist was fate, chance, method, or the impersonal "bank" which was supposed to represent them all; there was no individual

Scenes such as this were illustrated perhaps more frequently than they actually occurred.

opposition or rivalry; nobody challenged the decision of the croupier or dealer.

I remember a conversation at the door of one saloon which was as characteristic for its brevity as it was a type of the prevailing stoicism. "Hello!" said a departing miner, as he recognized a brother miner coming in. "When did you come down?" "This morning," was the reply. "Made a strike?" suggested the first speaker. "You bet!" said the other and passed in. I chanced an hour later to be at the same place as they met again—their relative positions changed. "Whar now?" said the incomer. "Back to the mines." "Cleaned out?" "You bet!" Not a word more explained a common situation.

My first youthful experience at those tables was an accidental one. I was watching roulette one evening, intensely absorbed in the mere movement of the players. Either they were so preoccupied with the game or I was really older-looking than my actual years, but a bystander laid his hand familiarly on my shoulder and said, as to an ordinary habitué, "Ef you're not chippin' in yourself, pardner, 'spose you *give me* a show." Now, I honestly believe that up to that moment I had no intention, nor even a desire, to try my own fortune. But in the embarrassment of the sudden address I put my hand in my pocket, drew out a coin, and laid it, with an attempt at carelessness, but a vivid consciousness that I was blushing, upon a vacant number. To my horror I saw that I had put down a large coin—the bulk of my possessions! I did not flinch, however. I think any boy who reads this will understand my feeling; it was not only my coin but my manhood at stake! I gazed with a miserable show of indifference at the players, at the chandelier—anywhere but at the dreadful ball spinning around the wheel.

There was a pause; the game was declared, the rake rattled up and down, but still I did not look at the table. Indeed, in my inexperience of the game and my embarrassment I doubt if I should have known if I had won or not. I had made up my mind that I should lose, but I must do so like a man, and, above all, without giving the least suspicion that I was a greenhorn. I even affected to be listening to the music. The wheel spun again; the game was declared, the rake was busy, but I did not move. At last the man I had displaced touched me on the arm and whispered, "Better make a straddle and divide your stake this time." I did not understand him, but as I saw he was looking at the board, I was obliged to look, too. I drew back dazed

Sampan coolies in the city streets were as common to San Francisco as the trade winds and gambling saloons.

and bewildered! Where my coin had lain a moment before was a glittering heap of gold.

My stake had doubled, quadrupled, and doubled again. I did not know how much then; I do not know now. It may have been not more than three or four hundred dollars but it dazzled and frightened me. "Make your game, gentlemen," said the croupier monotonously. I thought he looked at me—indeed, everybody seemed to be looking at me—and my companion repeated his warning. But here I must again appeal to the boyish reader in defense of my idiotic obstinacy. To have taken advice would have shown my youth. I shook my head—I could not trust my voice. I smiled, but with a sinking heart, and let my stake remain. The ball again sped around the wheel and stopped. There was a pause. The croupier indolently advanced his rake and swept my whole pile away with others into the bank! I had lost it all.

Perhaps it may be difficult for me to explain why I actually felt relieved, and even to some extent triumphant, but I seemed to have asserted my grown-up independence—possibly at the cost of reducing the number of my meals for days, but what of that! I was a man! I wish I could say that it was a lesson for me. I am afraid it was not. It was true that I did not gamble again, but then I had no especial desire to—and there was no temptation. I am afraid it was an incident without a moral. Yet it had one touch characteristic of the period which I like to remember. The man who had spoken to me I think suddenly realized at the moment of my disasterous coup the fact of my extreme youth. He moved toward the banker, and leaning over him whispered a few words. The banker looked up, half impatiently, half kindly—his hand straying tentatively toward the pile of coins. I instinctively knew what he meant, and summoning my determination, met his eyes with all the indifference I could assume, I turned and walked away....

At the time of these earlier impressions the Chinese had not yet become the recognized factors in the domestic and business economy for the city which they had come to be when I returned from the mines three years

later. Yet they
were even then a
more remarkable
and picturesque contrast
to the bustling, breathless and
brand-new life of San Francisco
than the Spaniard. The latter seldom
flaunted his faded dignity in the principle
thoroughfares. The Chinese were to be met everywhere. It was a common thing to see a long file of sampan coolies carrying their baskets slung between them
on poles, jostling a modern, well-dressed crowd in
Montgomery Street, or to get a whiff of their burned
punk in the side streets; while the road leading to their
temporary burial ground at Lone Mountain was lit-
tered with slips of colored paper scattered from their
funerals. They brought an atmosphere of the Arabian
Nights into the hard, modern civilization; their
shops—not always confined at that time to a Chinese
Quarter—were replicas of the bazaars of Canton and
Peking, with their quaint display of little dishes on
which tidbits of food delicacies were exposed for sale,
all of the dimensions and unreality of a doll's kitchen
or a child's housekeeping.

My wanderings were confined to the limits of the
city for the very good reason that there was little elsewhere to go. San Francisco was then bounded on one
side by the monotonously restless waters of the bay
and on the other by a stretch of equally restless and
monotonously shifting sand dunes as far as the Pacific
shore. Two roads penetrated this waste: one to Lone
Mountain—the cemetery; the other to the Cliff
House—happily described as "an eight-mile drive with
a cocktail at the end of it."

Nor was the humor entirely confined to this felici-
tous description. The Cliff House itself, half restau-
rant, half drinking saloon, fronting the ocean and the
Seal Rock where disporting seals were the chief object
of interest, had its own peculiar symbol. The decant-
ers, wineglasses and tumblers at the bar were all en-
graved in the old English script, with the legal initials

"L.S." (Locus Sigilli)—"the place of the seal."

On the other hand, Lone Mountain, a dreary promontory giving upon the Golden Gate and its striking sun-
sets, had little to soften its weird suggestiveness. As
the common goal of the successful and unsuccessful,
the carved and lettered shaft of the man who had made
a name and the staring blank headboard of the man
who had none climbed the sandy slopes together. I
have seen the funerals of the respectable citizen who
had died peacefully in his bed, and the notorious
desperado who had died "with his boots on," followed
by an equally impressive cortege of sorrowing friends,
and often the selfsame priest. But more awful than its
barren loneliness was the utter absense of peacefulness
and rest in this dismal promontory.

By some wicked irony of situation and climate it was
the personification of unrest and change. The incessant
trade winds carried its loose sands hither and thither,
uncovering the decaying coffins of early pioneers, to
bury the wreaths and flowers, laid on a grave of today,
under their obliterating waves. No tree to shade them
from the glaring sky above could live in those winds,
no turf would lie there to resist the encroaching sand
below. The dead were hurried and hustled even in their
graves by the persistent sun, the unremitting wind and
the unceasing sea. The departing mourner saw the con-
tour of the very mountain itself change with the shifting dunes as he passed, and his last look beyond rested
on the hurrying, eager waves forever hastening to the
Golden Gate.

If I were asked to say what one thing impressed me
as the dominant and characteristic note of San Francisco, I should say it was this untiring presence of sun
and wind and sea. They typified, even if they were not,
as I sometimes fancied, the actual incentive to the
fierce, restless life of the city. I could not think of San
Francisco without the trade winds; I could not imagine
its strange, incongruous multigenerous procession
marching to any other music. They were always there
in my youthful recollections; they were there in my

more youthful dreams of the past as the mysterious *vientes generales* that blew the Philippine galleons home.

For six months, they blew from the northwest, for six months from the southwest with unvarying persistency. They were there every morning, glittering in the equally persistent sunlight to chase the San Franciscan from his slumber; they were there at midday to stir his pulses with their beat; they were there again at night to hurry him through the bleak and flaring gas-lit streets to bed. They left their mark on every windward street or fence or gable, on the outlying sand dunes; they lashed the slow coasters home and hurried them to sea again; they whipped the bay into turbulence on their way to Contra Costa, whose level shoreland oaks

they had trimmed to windward as cleanly and sharply as with pruning shears. Untiring themselves, they allowed no laggards; they drove the San Franciscan from the wall against which he would have leaned, from the scant shade in which at noontide he might have rested. They turned his smallest fires into conflagrations and kept him ever alert, watchful and eager. In return, they scavenged his city and held it clean and wholesome; in summer they brought him the soft sea fog for a few hours to soothe his abraded surfaces; in winter they brought the rains and dashed the whole coast line with flowers, and the staring sky above it with soft, unwonted clouds. The winds were always there—strong, vigilant, relentless, material, unyielding, triumphant. (1900)

W.H.D. Koerner (1878-1938)

Through the history of California, colorful figures passed amid the constancy of the sun and the wind and the sea.

The Senator Remembers

Personal Recollections

of **William M. Stewart**

In 1908 a distinguished Senator who had represented Nevada in Congress for 29 years wrote for the Post *humorous recollections of early days in the gold fields and of his friendship with a transplanted Missourian.*

In the summer of 1850, only a few months after my arrival in California by way of the Isthmus, I was working a mining claim with a young man named Doctor Merrick. One morning I awoke to see a covered wagon with two oxen which had been unyoked and were grazing on a grassplot near a spring in the ravine below me. I soon discovered that a line had been drawn from the wagon to a clump of rocks, upon which were hung several female garments to dry.

Women were so scarce in California at that time that this was sufficient to arouse the whole camp. The "boys," as we were called, were scattered along the Coyote diggings for a distance of about four miles, and when anything unusual happened, the words, "Oh, Joe!" would be passed along the whole line.

When I saw the female garments I raised the usual alarm, "Oh, Joe!" and this called the attention of the miners on Buckeye Hill, where I was, to the clothesline which had attracted my attention. They gathered around on the hill, nearly surrounding the covered wagon and its contents.

The rush of the boys in the immediate vicinity to see the wonderful sight attracted those farther away, and, in less than ten minutes, two or three thousand young men were anxiously watching the wagon, clothesline

and mysterious lingerie. The man that belonged to the woman inside, in alarm, stuck his head out of a small tent beside the wagon. I assured him that no harm was intended, but that we were very anxious to see the lady who was the owner of the clothes. This aroused her curiosity sufficiently to induce her to pull the curtain of the tent aside so that her face could be discovered, but not fully seen.

I then proposed that we make a donation to the first lady who had honored our camp with a visit. I took from my camp a buckskin bag, used for the purpose of carrying gold, and invited the boys to contribute. They came forward with great eagerness and poured out of their sacks gold dust amounting to between two and three thousand dollars. Then I proposed to appoint a committee to wait on the lady and present it. The motion was unanimously carried, and one of the men appointed suggested that I be made chairman.

I took the sack of gold and went within about 30 feet of the tent and made as good a speech as I could to induce the lady to come out, assuring her that all the men about her were gentlemen, that they had seen no ladies for many, many months, and that the presence of one reminded them of their mothers and sweethearts at home. I told her the bag of gold was hers on condition that she would come out and claim it.

Her husband urged her to be brave, but, when she finally ventured about halfway, the cheers were so vociferous that she was scared and ran back.

She repeated this performance several times, and I kept moving slowly back far enough to get her away from the little tent so the boys could have a good view of her. I suppose half an hour was occupied with her running back and forth as the boys looked on in admiration, when I finally gave her the bag with all the good wishes of the camp. She

W.H.D. Koerner (1878-1938)

Another worthless claim—but miners were of hardy stock, and moved on to the next camp with high hopes.

The "cradle" processed large amounts of earth, was used extensively in the mining camps of California in the 1850s.

grabbed it and ran into the tent like a rabbit.

The next morning the wagon, oxen, man and owner of the female garments were gone, and we never heard of them in after life. It was no doubt well they hastened their departure, for in those days it was a common occurrence for the young wife coming to that country to be persuaded to forsake her husband on their arrival in the new camp.

The immigrants of 1850 included thousands of newly married young people whose wedding journey included all the hardships and privations of crossing the plains. These hardships made the men look rather rough and scrubby, and they were all miserably poor.

The women were young and after an opportunity to wash their faces, they looked more attractive— particularly to the miners, who had been deprived of female society for many months and had accumulated some money.

Such young men usually indulged in store clothes and spruced up. The contrast between them and the immigrant who had just crossed the plains was very marked. These young men were very anxious for ladies' society, and at once paid court to the young married women, and in a very large number of cases they were able to persuade the ladies that they were not fully appreciated at the time of their marriage, and that they had made a mistake in marrying beneath them.

Usually, the husband, naturally enough, became very jealous and tried to prevent the sociability which sprung up between his wife and the spruce young miner. Then there would be angry words between the husband and the wife's admirer, which frequently resulted in blows, and if the husband got the worst of it his wife would have no further use for him. The miner would propose marriage if a divorce could be obtained. Extreme cruelty was given as the reason for the divorce. The intended bridegroom was always a ready witness to swear to a case of extreme cruelty. . . .

When I first knew Sam Clemens he was a reporter on the *Territorial Enterprise*, which was otherwise a very reputable paper, published in Virginia City, and his brother Orion Clemens, was a respectable young gentleman and well liked.

Clemens had a great habit of making fun of the young fellows and the girls, and wrote ridiculous pieces about parties and other social events, to which he was never invited. After a while he went over to Carson City and touched up the people over there, and got everybody down on him. I thought he had faded from our midst forever, but he drifted back to Virginia City in a few weeks. The boys got together and said they would give a party, and invite Clemens to it, and make him feel at home, and respectable, and decent, and kindly, and generous, and loving and considerate of the feelings of others. I could have warned them, but I didn't.

Clemens went to that party and danced with the prettiest girls, and monopolized them, and enjoyed himself, and made a good meal, and then shoved over to the *Enterprise* office and wrote the whole thing up.

He lambasted that party for all the English language would allow, and if any of the guests were unfortunate enough to be awkward, or have big feet or a wart on the nose, Clemens did not forget it. He fairly strained his memory.

Of course, this made the boys angry and they decided to get even. There was a stage that ran from Carson to Virginia City, and Clemens was a passenger on it one night. The boys laid in wait, and when the stage lumbered by a dark lonely spot they swooped out, and upset it, and turned it upside down and dragged him out, and threw him into a canyon, and broke up his port-manteau, and threw that in on top of him.

He was the scaredest man west of the Missis-sippi; but the next morning, when he crawled back to town, and it was light, and safe, he began to swell a little and pretty soon he was bragging about his narrow escape. By and by he began to color it up some, and add details that he had perhaps overlooked at first, until he made out that he had been in one of the most desperate stage robberies in the history of the West, and it was a pretty poor story that he could not lug *that* one into, by the nape of the neck, sort of casually like.

After that incident he drifted away, and I thought he had been hanged, or elected to Congress or something like that. One thing I was was confi-dent that he would come to no good end, but I have heard of him from time to time, since then, and I understand that he has now settled down and become quite respectable, after all. (1908)

Stagecoach drivers rode "shotgun" to protect the passengers from hold-up—natural hazards were problem enough.

Henry and the Golden Mine

A Story by Stephen Vincent Benét

It's where you find it, and that's just the trouble. There never was a truer word said. You can get all your Eastern geologists with their hammers and their spectacles and set them running all over the state of California. But the gold's the gold. You're as likely to come across it, looking for a stray mule—that's what made the Four Brothers' claim. And you'll find it and lose it and find it. You remember the kid with the slingshot on the wagon train. He was peppering all and sundry with some nice hard pebbles he'd picked up, and when they took away his slingshot they found out what kind of pebbles they were. Only then he couldn't remember where he'd come across them, and three men died of thirst in the desert, trying to locate the spot. But it never was found, and never will be—wasn't meant to be found, I guess. And then, there's the Mother Lode.

Oh, any professor will tell you that it doesn't exist, and couldn't. There couldn't be such a thing—where the vein runs wide as a street down into the heart of the mountain, and you could walk around blindfolded and it wouldn't make any difference to your luck. But it's been seen and located, or so they say. Except, they say it's guarded too; though I wouldn't like to specify by who or what. I've been alone in the mountains myself. And maybe the voices you hear are all inside your own head. But, again, they might not be. I'm not going to look for it, anyway—I'm not so young as I was. Though nat-

urally, now and then, when you think of it, you get a hankering. But they say—the best informed—that only a fool can find it. And I'm not Henry Pink.

He wasn't really a fool, either. Just kind of innocent and eager and enthusiastic. He'd come around the Horn to the gold fields, but it hadn't changed him a mite. He still looked as if he washed his face every morning because his mother told him to, and a body couldn't be with him more than half an hour without knowing all about him—how he came from Laertes, New York, and was bound to make his pile because of a girl named Hester that he wanted to marry. She was a girl with quite a lot of forehead, who wrote poetry for the paper, but—as he was apt to remark—she was full of soul. It looked more like dyspepsia to me, in the tintype he had of her, but he thought different. There'd been another girl, Amy Frothingham, but the trouble with her was, she was golden-haired but fickle. Yes, I'm telling it to you just the way he told it to me.

That's the kind of boy he was, and you couldn't help it. He even carried a piece of Hester's poetry around with him. It was kind of worn at the edges, but he was perfectly willing to read it out loud. It was called To a Distant Friend and it began "How drear now rolls old Hudson's stream," and went on about sweet reunion in the by and by. Hester generally specialized in willows by a grave and white-robed angels coming for the souls

Panning was the most common method employed by the 80,000 prospectors who came to California in 1849.

of the departed, so this was a pretty cheerful piece, for her. It wouldn't have struck my fancy, exactly, as a keepsake, but I wasn't Henry Pink.

You couldn't help liking him, that was the difficulty. But after you'd seen a little of him, you got kind of awestruck at the inscrutable ways of Providence. You can talk about guardian angels, but one wouldn't have been enough for Henry. There must have been a whole squad of them, and all of them overworked. I remember when he first showed up at the diggings. He had a big, old-fashioned pepperbox of a gun and a regular fancy outfit, washbowl and all. He looked like a picture of a miner in an emigrant's guide. Well, I'd just come out of the Last Chance and I was still wiping my mouth, when he stepped up to me.

"I beg your pardon," he said, "but I am a stranger in these parts and would greatly appreciate your directing me to accommodation for the night." Yes, he still talked like that—he talked just like a book. I took one look at him, but I didn't laugh. It hurt me a little not to, but we've all been young once, and you could see the eagerness sticking out all over him.

"Well, young man," I said, "the question of accommodation in our thriving little metropolis is, if I may say so, a vexed one. For instance, there's Barney's Imperial Palace Tavern."

"Where's that?" he said.

"You go on down the trail and you'll see it," I said. "You see something that looks like a cross between an Injun wickiup and a motherless circus tent. That's Barney's."

"And are Mr. Barney's charges reasonable?" said he.

"Very reasonable," said I. "He was charging eight dollars, dust, for half a bunk, washing excluded. Of course, that was yesterday, and prices may have riz. But there's just one thing—don't let him bed you down with a Texas man. They're apt to be born with spurs, and they rake when they get nightmares."

"Born with spurs?" he said, with his eyes as big and innocent as saucers.

"Born or growed," I said. "It comes of drinking Rio Grande water. Interesting phenomenon."

"I shall write that home to Hester," he said. "Her father's editor of the Laertes Item, and he will be very interested. The spurs, I should judge, would be of the same substance as the fingernails?"

"They claim chilled steel," I said, "but I never dehorned one to find out. And then, of course, if you don't like Barney's—well, there's the whole territory of California to bed out in."

"I admit expense is an item," he said. "On the other hand, I am anxious to form connections"—and damned if he didn't shove me a little printed card. It said, THE LAERTES MINING AND DEVELOPMENT CO., HENRY PINK, PRESIDENT AND TREASURER, and it was then I began to worry about his guardian angels. He looked at me sort of anxious.

"It is not a very large company," he said, "but my

good friend, Reuben Plummer, the son of our leading undertaker, has associated himself financially with me in the enterprise. Also Judge Hannafield and Hester's father. In fact, he put up my passage money, and I shall always be grateful to him, for he said it was cheap at the price. But it puts a large responsibility upon my shoulders. Naturally, I wish to find my first bonanza as rapidly as possible. Bonanza is the correct term, is it not? Yet, perhaps, it would be wise to seek some accommodation first; the trip has been somewhat fatiguing"—and he kind of swayed on his feet.

Well, I heaved a sigh at the thought of it, but I told him he'd better bunk with me—at least for the night. I couldn't do otherwise. If I'd let him go on alone, he might have been eaten by a jack rabbit, or so I figured. I can't say I was living in the altitudes of luxury—the roof hadn't been mended since the Mexican fell through it. But when I got some food inside the youngster, he seemed very pleased and grateful. He told me a lot more about Hester and showed me her poetry. And then, before I was even waked up, in the morning he went out and jumped Horse Mason's claim.

He came steaming back to the cabin with his coat-tails flying. I'd heard the shots, but I never was a person to borrow trouble. But I tell you, he didn't know anything. He'd just gone out with his washbowl and picked a likely piece of ground.

"And then what happened?" I said.

"Why," he said, "a very nice old gentleman with a white beard began shooting around me."

"That's Horse Mason," I said. "And it's the first time in human history he's been called a nice old gentleman. Was he drunk?"

"Oh, no," he said kind of shocked, as he fingered the holes in his hat. "He seemed quite in possession of his faculties, though very angry. If he had only allowed me to explain—"

"Explain?" I said. "Couldn't you see the claim was staked?"

"I did observe some little sticks," he said, "but—"

Well, then, I sat him down and talked to him like a Dutch uncle. I must have talked to him an hour. Then I went to pacify Horse, which took some time. And when I got back the youngster had dug a two-foot hole in the ground right back of the cabin and was making the dirt fly. I just stared at him.

"All right," I said. "You've had your exercise. Now fill it up."

"I thought I saw indications of gold," he said.

"Listen," I said. "You forget anything you ever heard—or read in the Laertes Item—about indications. Do you think I'd have been squatting here for a month—and ten men before me—with the gold right under our noses, and not know it? You fill up that hole, and do it fast, or I'll beat you to death with a shovel," I

said, because I was getting a little roused. "Furthermore, I'll take that pepperbox gun away from you and make you eat it. And furthermore and like-wise——"

Well, I may have gone on for a bit, but I wanted to make an impression. And apparently I did, for the youngster did as I told him. All the same, I saw him stow away a sample of the dirt in a little leather bag he had. But I didn't let on I'd seen. It didn't do any harm, and I knew he'd forget about it the next day.

That was how we got to be partners and, in some ways, I've never had a better one. He was good-humored and a hard worker, and we struck on a little pocket that panned out pretty well. Not any bonanza, you understand, but enough to make you feel good. Shucks, he insisted on giving me a note for a hundred shares of stock in the Laertes Mining and Development Company, just because I'd showed him the ropes. Well, it didn't mean anything to me, but I didn't want to hurt his feelings, so I took it and thanked him. Then the news came along of the new strike up at Puma, and half the camp went crazy. I'd been in those rushes before and it didn't impress me much. You wear your legs out getting there, and then you find all the good ground's located. But my youngster was wild to go.

I should have gone with him, I guess, and I certainly hated to see him leave. But he was shaping up well, and you can't wet-nurse a youngster beyond a certain point.

An idle dreamer?? Probably another prospector turned farmer. The mountains called to men, enticing them with legends of the Mother Lode—a fictional vein of gold protected by the gods, said to be incredulously rich.

It isn't fair. So I said I'd take care of things at my end, and if Puma really panned out he could send me word. It sounded more impressive, put like that. Myself, I thought he wouldn't find anything, and that might knock some sense in him. But I was wrong.

He never got there at all; he got lost in the mountains. It took a special talent to do that, with hundreds of men all going the same way, but he managed it. He thought he'd take a short cut, you see—a short cut, when he didn't even know enough to follow water downhill. Well, he had a burro with him, and grub, so that wasn't so bad. But the country wasn't exactly like Laertes, New York, and, once he got off the trail, he kept wandering in and in. It's easy to do in those ranges.

It wasn't so bad the first day or the first couple of days. He found water and grass all the way—or the burro found them for him. At first he was scared of Indians; then, after a while Indians would have been a relief. There were coyotes and deer and such; he didn't like the coyotes at night, and yet, in a way, they were company. But it seemed to him, as he went deeper and deeper into the mountains, that the animals got fewer and fewer. Till, finally, when he'd pitch camp and light his fire, the night would be dead still, without a sound in it, except for the wind in the trees and the little noise of his burro, stirring around. It was then that he began to talk to Hester. He knew perfectly well she wasn't there, but he talked to her all the same.

He talked to her because he'd begun to wonder if there'd ever been a town called Laertes, or a state called New York, or even a likely youngster that his friends called Henry Pink. He could see the town perfectly

Burros, hardy creatures able to withstand extreme conditions, have saved men's lives by leading them to water.

well, when he thought of it; see the livery stable and the church and the old hand press in the Item office and Hester's father, with the little white tufts of hair that grew out of his ears. He could even see Amy Frothingham, sitting in the third row at Sabbath school. He could see it all just as plain as a picture in Harper's Weekly, but it didn't seem real to him at all.

He told Hester all about this and how queer it was. And at first that was a consolation, but after a while it got so that all she'd do would be to recite poetry to him. He never thought he'd really get tired of her poetry. But he found he did—particularly of "How drear now rolls old Hudson's stream." Finally he got so he'd carry a handful of rocks in his pocket, and whenever Hester started in about the rolling stream he'd chunk one at her. He hated to do it and always apologized. But it seemed to be the one way to fix her.

He'd been having a pretty bad time with Hester,

when he finally saw the campfire at the end of the valley. At first he was perfectly convinced that the campfire wasn't there either. He was so convinced that he meant to walk straight through it and show them. But he didn't, because the burro balked.

The old man on the other side of the fire didn't even move. He was cooking bacon in a skillet, and he just said, "*Buenas noches, amigo.* You have come a long way." I guess it was the smell of the bacon that made Henry feel dizzy. He'd meant to eat regular, but he'd spent too much time, lately, throwing rocks at Hester to think about his meals. Anyhow, it got black in front of him, and he sat down.

When he got back his senses the burro had its pack off and was munching away, and the old man had a plate of bacon all ready for him. It was only after he'd eaten and the life had begun to come back to him that he really noticed the old man.

He was brown and he looked Mexican—dressed Mexican, too, for his vest had gold buttons on it and he had a Mexican knife. But again you couldn't tell.

His voice was kind of slow and stately, but he talked American. And in spite of his hair being white, his eyes were young and alive and black as coal.

"Eat, *amigo*; I am glad to see you at last," he said to Henry Pink, and nodded his head.

"Well, that's very friendly of you, sir, and I'm glad to hear a human voice again," said Henry. "But I don't see how you could have been exactly expecting me."

"What is expectation?" said the old man, and he rolled a thin brown cigarette between his fingers. "The tree does not expect the lightning nor the fish the hook. Yet the two come together in time, when there is a purpose"—and he smiled in a queer way.

"Now, that's very handsome talk," said Henry. "I like to hear a man talk like that. My father-in-law would be interested too; he edits the Laertes Item and he's a well-educated man. At least, he isn't my father-in-law yet, but he's going to be. At least, if Hester will ever quit reciting poetry." And he reached in his pocket for a rock. But he didn't use it, for Hester wasn't there any more—just him and the old man and the bright fire. He passed his hand over his forehead.

"Excuse me," he said. "I guess I've been talking wild. I could see her there, just as plain as print. But now she's gone back to Laertes."

"What you see may be so and what you do not see may be so," said the old man. "Permit me to introduce myself"—and he rolled out a long, liquid name. It began with "Don Felipe" and went on for quite a spell, till it ended in something like "Alcantara"—or that's what Henry made of it.

"Delighted to make your acquaintance, sir," said Henry, and reached in his pocket. "This will explain my own interests and activities," he said. "As I said before—or maybe I didn't—we mean to call our first bonanza the Hester. But it's all there on the card."

The old man took the card—kind of dog-eared by now—and looked at it.

"The gold," he said; "always the gold." And his face was stern in the firelight. "Well, young man, you were born to be fortunate. Otherwise you would not have come to Lost Mountain. But now we will sleep, I think"—and he rolled up in his serape and shut his eyes.

It came upon Henry, for a minute, that he mightn't be so harmless as he looked and that maybe this wasn't such a good place to be. But then he found his own eyes were shutting and, before he knew it, it was day.

When he woke up, the pack was already on the burro and the coffee hot on the fire.

"We have a long way to go," said the old man. "You had better eat, my friend."

"Excuse me," said Henry Pink, "but I don't know where we're going."

"Why, to find the gold, of course. Is that not what you have come for?" said the old man, and after they'd had their victuals he led the way.

It was pretty country, but lonesome, there in the high ranges. Henry felt the loneliness all day, like a weight on the back of his neck. He didn't mention it to the old man because he felt, somehow, that the old man was part of the loneliness and it suited him. He went ahead leading the burro, and he was perfectly real, and yet he made Henry wonder. That night they camped on the slope of Lost Mountain itself. No, I can't tell you where it was, though I know the range.

After they'd eaten, the old man lit one of his thin brown cigarettes. He gave one to Henry, too, and the smoke made Henry feel queer.

"Now, this gold you were talking about," said Henry, kind of shyly. "I don't want to seem inquisitive, but since you mentioned the fact——"

"You will see it soon enough," said the old man. "I know how you feel; I, too, have been young and greedy. It is for that reason that I am not allowed to die."

"I don't think I quite caught what you were saying," said Henry Pink.

"It is very simple," said the old man, watching the red end of his cigarette. "We were all strong greedy men, from Hernando Cortes himself to yellow-haired Alvarado. We meant to have the gold, and we got it—six hundred thousand marks of pure gold we wrung from Montezuma at one blow, besides the precious stones. Yet we loaded him with irons and burned his servants alive. No, the wrong was not all on our side—we had seen the human hearts smoke on the altars of the city. But one does not repay wrong with wrong."

"I can't understand what you're talking about," said Henry Pink, with a cold sweat beginning to break out upon him. "At least I hear the words, but they don't make sense to me. Because if you're talking about what I think you're talking about——"

"I am talking about the men who took the city Tenochtitlan and survived the

Noche Triste—the Night of Dolor," said the old man. "You are new conquistadores, you *yanquis*. But we were conquistadores before."

"But you can't—I mean it can't be—I mean I've heard about it and it was centuries ago," said Henry.

"Three hundred and thirty years and more since we burnt the ships," said the old man. "I remember how bright the flame was—bright under a blue sky."

Henry looked at him again, and his hands looked as brown and withered as the stump of his cigarette. It gave Henry an uncanny feeling—the hands were so brown and withered and the eyes so black and bright.

"You couldn't—it ain't in nature," he said, but he said it in a whisper.

"It is not in nature, no—wolves and bears do not tear each other for pieces of bright metal. But it was in our hearts," said the old man, with a fearful smile. "If we had not been bold, greedy men, we would not have won an empire. And I, my friend, I was as bold as Alvarado—as bold and greedy as he, and as good a sword. I did not have his luck—he had the luck of the devil—but in all other ways we were equal. I remember those days; no gold we got was enough for us; if the whole round earth had been turned into a ball of gold, we would have beaten upon it with our fists and cried, 'More, more!' Yet was I no worse than the rest—not till the torture of Guatemotzin."

"Who was he?" said Henry Pink.

"He was a man," said the old man, his eyes glowing. "Yes, heathen or not, he was a man—even upon the rack. Have you ever seen a man upon the rack, my young friend? It is a curious experience. The cacique we tortured with Guatemotzin groaned and cried aloud. 'Do you think I am lying upon a bed of roses?' said Guatemotzin, the emperor, and that was all that he said, no matter how we tightened the cords."

"I thought you said Montezuma was emperor," said Henry Pink.

"He had been," said the old man. "If Guatemotzin had been emperor when we landed, not one of us would have survived the Noche Triste. Montezuma was a woman, but not this man. But we caught Guatemotzin at last, and it was I who struck him across the face and bade him tell us where the gold was. Yes, I did that, even as he lay upon the rack. And for that our little priest rebuked me. He called on my blood and my honor, and said it was shame in a conquistador to strike a tortured man. A bold man, that little priest. Then he held up the cross in front of me to stay me, but I struck the cross to the ground."

There was a long silence then, and Henry Pink didn't say anything.

"Yes, it was so," said the old man. "I shall not forget it. For the tortured man writhed his own lips then, and I

The Conquistadors took back to Europe stories of fabulous wealth and stolen gold.

could hear him speak words. 'The white man denies his own God,' he said to the little priest, and the priest silently picked up his crucifix from the dust. 'Do you claim this man for your God?' said the tortured man again, and again the priest kept silence. I felt the others fall away from me then—yes, even the roughest and the wildest, who had marched and fought at my side.

" 'Then I claim this man for our gods,' cried Guatemotzin, Emperor of Mexico, from the rack where we had stretched him. 'I claim him for the gold he worships, that he look for it continually, wishing to die, but unable to die, as I wish to die today—until he can find a man of another race who will accept his gold and its burden.' There was no more said than that, and I just laughed in his face. But when the torture was over and Guatemotzin dead, men began to look upon me strangely. Even Alvarado, who had been my friend."

"Well, sir, that's a mighty queer story," said Henry Pink. "And I don't say you done right. But still, if you got the gold——"

"That was what I thought," said the old man. "It seemed to me a good bargain. It seemed so, indeed, till I found that I could not die. Oh, I had many escapes, but the arrow would not pierce nor the ball strike. I was with Alvarado in Guatemala; I have searched for the cities of Cibola, the golden cities; I have wandered the length of the land. For, always, I must look for the gold, as Guatemotzin, the emperor, had said. And the men I knew died, and their sons died, and their sons' sons, but still there was no death for me. So, at last I came here, for here, surely, was a land without gold and the curse of

gold—a pleasant, smiling land, where a man might live in peace till death tapped his shoulder."

He shook his head.

"And so it was," he said. "So it was, for many years. Nor was it I who unloosed the secret, though I knew of it. You *yanquis* think you know California, but it is not the California I know. Oh, the good, lazy, sun-warmed land, the fine horses, the grapes on the vine! But now that is over."

He rose.

"We will look at the gold now," he said. "You scrabble in the streams like children for a pennyweight here and there. But here is the lode and the treasure—the mother of it all. I have kept the secret a long time—that I have done, at least, for the sake of the sun-warmed land. But now it matters no more and it is time I had rest."

He picked up a pine torch and led the way to a heap of logs and underbrush. They worked for two hours, cleaning the stuff away; and when they'd done, there was a big black hole in the side of the mountain. Don Felipe held up his torch.

"The shaft is a natural one," he said. "It was covered by a rock slide when I found it. Let us go in."

They went in, and the air was sweet, so there

Gold and Greed: the surrounding myth, its manifestations and the dilemma of mortal man—will he succumb?

must have been some sort of vent in the side of the mountain.

"Where's the gold, old man?" said Henry, trembling all over.

"You are walking over it and under it; you are walking through it and around it," said the old man mysteriously, in kind of a singsong voice, waving his torch.

And as he waved it around, the red flame lit up the rough walls of the enormous rock chamber till they seemed all in a sparkling fire.

Henry took one look around. He wasn't educated or a geologist, but he could believe his own eyes. And this wasn't a placer or a pocket. It was Golconda. The veins ran wide as a street and they seemed to go down forever—quartz rotten with gold, moth-eaten with gold, loaded and crammed with pure gold. Henry caught his breath.

"The Mother Lode—the thing that could not be true," said the old man. "And nobody has ever seen it but you and I."

"Can I—do you mind if I——" said Henry, and his voice was shaking.

"That is why you are here," said the old man sadly. He passed Henry a little hammer. "Strike where you will," he said. "It is all the same."

"Oh, Laertes, New York!" said Henry, kind of prayerful. "Oh, Hester, and won't you be proud of me!"

Then he went about with his hammer, tapping the walls. He knocked off a sample here and a sample there, and when he had the stuff in his hand he didn't believe it. And then he did believe it, and it made him feel extremely queer.

He was standing there, in dirty pants and a ragged shirt, and yet he was a millionaire. He was richer than Astor or the Barings or anybody. He was richer than a body could be and still stay reasonable. And the joy of it flooded through him till he thought it would stop his heart. But then, being a sensible youngster, he calmed down and began to consider.

Naturally the old man would want half of it, but, even so, he'd still be rich. He didn't take any stock in the old man's story about living three hundred years and being one of the conquistadores. That was just the loony ramblings of a half-crazy Mexican prospector. But, after all, the old bezabor had found the claim, and Henry meant to deal square with him. It seemed an awful lot, when you started thinking about it—half the biggest treasure on earth for a crazy old coot who wouldn't know what to do with it. But Henry had always been an honest boy. He wondered how much stock in the Laertes Mining and Development Company he'd have to give the old fellow. Then he looked at the samples in his hand again and wondered if he couldn't buy him off with a flat cash payment. When you thought of it, five thousand dollars would be a whale of a lot of money for an old man like that—more than he'd ever seen in his life, probably. Only Henry didn't have the five thousand dollars.

"Are you satisfied?" said the old man. He had his back turned to Henry, but his voice kind of

boomed against the rocks with an ominous echo.

"Why wouldn't a man be satisfied?" said Henry in a queer voice. He scraped a flake of gold from the quartz with the edge of his fingernail—it was as easy as that. And the old man still had his back turned. He hadn't said a thing about relatives, but then, he wouldn't have any—not if he was three hundred years old. And three hundred years was a long enough time for anybody. Henry picked up the hammer from where he'd dropped it. It felt good and solid in his hand. He could see the old man falling, and then it would be finished, and Henry Pink would be the richest man in the world.

"Are you satisfied, Guatemotzin, my enemy?" said the old man, as if he were talking to himself. "It has been a long, weary time."

And then, with the sound of the voice, Henry knew he couldn't do it. He knew he couldn't do it at all. He felt the hammer fall out of his hand and heard it clatter on the rock.

"Say," he said, "if I could interest you in a first-rate straight proposition. I don't mean to jump anybody's claim—I did that once, but that was because I didn't know. But this is the Laertes Mining and Development Company and I'm president and treasurer. I've got to keep fifty-one per cent of the stock, you see, because of Hester. In spite of her writing poetry. But I guess we could come to an arrangement."

"You are young and strong," said the old man. "It would be so much easier for you to kill me."

"Oh, a whole lot easier, not to speak of more convenient," said Henry earnestly. "But, you see, I don't think Amy Frothingham would like it. She's a flirt and

Man and beast are one in their mutual fight against the elements of nature.

she's fickle, and I don't know why I'm thinking of her instead of Hester, but I figure she wouldn't like me to do a
thing like that. And then there's my friend Reb Plummer. Well, you might think an undertaker——but Reb's
a sensitive fellow—and I don't think he would either.
And I'd certainly hate to ruin Reb's opinion of me—he's
one of the best-thought-of people in Laertes. And then
there's Judge Hannafield—not that I care so much
what the judge thinks, but still——Oh, for God's sake!"
he said. "Will you come out of this cave? It's rich as all
get out, but I don't like one thing about it!"

The old man looked at him and smiled. Henry always
said it was a wonderful thing, that smile.

"You may go, my son," said the old man. "For that
was the second thing that was said to me. I was to live
till I found a man who would take my burden of guilt,
and with it the gold, or a boy who would refuse them
both. I thought it would be the first way.
But I was wrong. Oh, my California!" he
said. "My fine, lazy high-hearted land!
They will dig in your entrails for the gold
that ruins them, but I shall be at peace. Yes,
my young friend, go!"

Even so, right until he'd got back to the
campfire, Henry thought the old man was
following him. But when he woke the next
morning, there was only his own burro,
cropping, and the ashes of the fire. And
when he went back to the mountains, there was
just a big slide of rock where he figured the hole
must have been. Then he remembered he'd thought
he'd heard thunder in the night. So he put up a pile of
stones, left his Sunday-school medal under them to
show he'd been there, and moseyed.

At least, that's the way he told it when he got back to
Lone Tree. I hardly recognized him at first, to tell you
the truth. He was all over whiskers, for one thing. But it
was more than that. He'd gone out a boy, but he'd come
back a man. And he told his story like a man, in spite of
the wildness.

"No, I wouldn't believe it myself," he said in the end.
"But, you see, I've got evidence." And he fished out a
leather bag.

"That's real color," I said, looking at the samples.
"But I thought you said it was a quartz formation."

"That's right," he said, and then a curious expression
came over his face. "But that isn't the bag," he said. "It
isn't the right bag. The one I brought from the mountains was canvas. I ought to know. This here's just that
worthless dirt I scrabbled up behind the cabin the first
day you took me in. I can't tell you why I kept it—sort of
souvenir, maybe."

"Worthless dirt!" said I. "Oh, for God's sake, where's
my pan?" Well, it didn't take two minutes to show us
what we had. And I hadn't even bothered to stake

the place. But when I got through we were protected,
even if I did have to warn Horse Mason off with a
shotgun. We took sixteen thousand dollars in dust
right out of that back yard, and it nearly drove the
old man crazy. Well, don't ask me what I did with mine.
But a year or so later I paid my last two dollars for a letter at the express office. And worth it, at that, because
it said:

Laertes, N.Y.
January 18th, 1852.

Dear Friend: I hope this finds you as it leaves me, in
the best of health and spirits and also a married man.
Not to Hester, however, my dear friend, though I know
this will surprise. But on returning to Laertes, I found
out that a sympathy had sprung up between Hester and
my friend, Reb Plummer, due chiefly to a mutual interest in graves. In such circumstances there is nought
for a man to do but bow his head to the inscrutable decrees of destiny, which is just
as well—my never being able to feel quite
the same toward Hester since throwing those rocks at her to stop her poetry. While Amy Pink, nee Frothingham, is in every respect a pearl of
womanhood, and, to tell you the truth,
it was a misunderstanding with her that
drove me to Hester in the first place. Amy
sends her warmest regards to "my old
friend and partner" and extends, as do
I, the most cordial of invitations to visit
us in our home when you come East.
With which, wishing you every success and lots of
"dust," I remain,

Your true friend, HENRY PINK.

(Ex-President, Laertes Mining and Development
Company, present ed. and prop, Laertes Item, having
bought out Hester's father, who was anxious to sell.)

P.S.: We intend to call our first offspring after my
old partner.

Well, that's the story—and you can believe it or
otherwise, but I've talked to men who've got lost in
those ranges. They all say there's something queer
about them, once you start going in and in. And there
was a sheepherder once; he got lost and his sheep got
lost, and finally he got to a place where everything was
very still and quiet. Well, then, he got raving about
how spirits came out of the mountain and warned him
away. But he did bring something back with him. It
was an old Sunday-school medal, and it was all rusted
and tarnished. But you could still make out some of the
letters and they said "—OR G—OD —ONDUC—,
H——RY —INK." But when I asked him just where
he'd found it, he didn't make a word of sense. (1939)

Playing by the Rules

Memoirs of an Unknown Gambler

I was born and raised in a gold-mining camp of the high Sierras of California. I thrived among surroundings of chance, for even as a boy I saw men each day stake everything they had for gold. Some toiled far beneath the surface of the earth, by the dim light of a candle. Others, by the light of pitch-wood fires, played fierce streams of water against gravel banks through the long hours of the night, their oiled clothes dripping from the flashing spray. Guards with rifles patrolled the lines of flume where the precious metal reposed.

The first hour of winter dawn and the last hour of light saw scores of lonely miners on scores of mountain streams sluicing tons of earth for their ounce of gold. Then as the freshets receded and their labors relaxed, the prospectors came to the larger towns with their pouches of gold. Here they mingled with the owners of the hydraulic claims, their workmen and the men from the deep-drift gravel and quartz mines. For months their life had been a hazardous one, for accidents were frequent; and rolling rocks, caving banks, premature blasts, whirling hydraulic monitors, slips beneath the surface and other forms of sudden death exacted their steady toll. Now came their period of relaxation. Moreover, California in those days was known as the land of many bachelors. In the early days of that state there were few women, and the men planned to go East when

they made their stake. As a result, when they came down from the hills the bright lamps of the saloons and dance halls, the stimulus of liquor, the stacks of gold and silver behind the games of chance stirred these lonely men to reckless spending.

So, even as a small boy, I saw these rough, bearded men laughingly stack their hard-earned gold on the green cloth for another fling at chance. Gold and silver were the lure of their lives, and no other form of money was allowed on the gambling tables. I was 15 when I first saw a piece of currency. I would watch for hours with wildly beating heart as the gold and silver coins slid back and forth across the poker table.

When the miners played among themselves it was a fraternal affair, for the winners would stake the losers at the game's end. But like a pack of hungry wolves around a flock of sheep, the miners were constantly dogged by card sharps. Flushed by success in games with fellow miners, it was not hard to induce them to sit in games with other players. Honest in their own dealings, they were easy marks for the crooked gamblers.

It stirred my blood and strongly appealed to some element in my nature to see prospectors and miners daily risk life and limb for gold and then recklessly hazard it all on a turn of the card. So at an early age I found myself following in their footsteps. I listened

with greedy ears as the forty-niners told their marvelous tales of rich gold strikes, lost mines, big poker games, lynchings and desperate fights of the early California days. Yet, strange to tell in spite of the fact that cards were barred from our home by both my parents, very religious people, the tales of gambling held for me the strongest appeal of all.

As I grew older I worked at the many different methods of gold mining, panned the creeks, cradled a rocker, ground-sluiced, and finally worked in the hydraulic mines and carried a candle on hundreds of shifts thousands of feet below the surface of the earth. A portion of all my earnings went to the poker games, and card playing became a passion. I made the usual round of losings and winnings of the average player, and, of course, in the long run was always behind the game. However, I must have shown some aptitude above the majority of green players, for I was not out of my teens when an old-time California gambler offered me a position as dealer of the poker game in his saloon.

Plunging Jim—that was his nickname—the man for whom I worked, was a square old fellow. He had won

several fortunes while sober, for he was a tough poker player, but would make big losings when drinking. The last I ever heard of him was in the boom days of Dawson City, when he sat in a poker game with thousands of dollars in gold stacked before him. He was then 64 years old, but game as ever. Jim gave me much good advice, the best of which was that if I learned to play nothing but square cards I would be able to beat the crooked gamblers. However, I would have to learn every form of cheating so as to know what the crooked players were trying to hand me.

"Their money is a gift if you can dicker them down to square cards," he would say. "Keep your head working all the time. Spit in front of you and not behind," were some of his instructions.

We played old-style California poker; no joker, no straights, table stakes, and did not draw to flushes. Ordinarily it was a small game, 25-cent ante and no limit. Sometimes the game got fast. Then Jim would take my place and tell them to do all the plunging they wished, for he would be with them at the finish. I made big money right from the start, and Jim soon gave me

An aptitude for gambling was nurtured. Though mastered by a few, it was a skill respected by many.

gone, and deep, expensive mining methods were necessary. So there had developed a second generation of restless spirits who were forever lured on by visions of yellow coins stacked high on the gaming tables. Their methods of obtaining the refined product showed the same degree of courage and perseverance that marked their forebears' search for the crude metal, but their lives lacked the honesty and toil.

I soon became restless at Jim's and wanted to drift here, there, anywhere, just so long as I was on the move. So, after six months' training under the watchful eye of old Jim, I decided that I was keen enough to go on the road. Jim shook his head and grinned when I told him that I was going away for a while. He was a wise old bird and knew my finish. Being quite flush, I dolled up in fancy clothes and purchased a real diamond. I was on parade; I wanted people to know I was a gambler. Later experience taught me to try to convince people I was anything but that.

My first stop was at Bakersfield, California. Through some freak of good fortune I left there several days later over a hundred dollars winner. Flushed with success, I headed for Los Angeles, then a city of forty or fifty thousand population and more Eastern in manner than any place in the West.

I soon found a draw-poker game running on First Street, east of Main, and so I lit and began proving to them at once that I was a gambler. Whenever a fellow stuck his nose in a pot I plowed back at him. If one of them ever got a showdown for his money it was because he had all of it in the center of the table. I won over $200 in a few hours, this being a large winning for the size of the game. Later I realized that several factors were in my favor that day. I was playing uncommonly lucky, the game was the square, and I had landed on a bunch of timid poker players and boosters. For the next three days I continued to beat the game, but for smaller sums.

The afternoon of the third day the best poker player that I had noted in the games followed me out and said to me, "Kid, you've got a snap; you are too fast for us; we can't beat you. You have broke me along with the rest. I guess I know a real poker player when I see one."

I swelled up like a poisoned pup and slipped him a ten instead of the five that he asked for.

That evening I noticed that I was playing with different opponents; also that there was more money on the table and I was not getting away with my spectacular playbacks. I later learned that the house staked a couple of real poker players, and some of the top-notch gamblers hearing of the kid with a bank roll had dropped in for their portion. The game was not a crooked

a half interest in the game. Jim fed the poker bug in my brain, yet from his point of view it was an honest move. He looked on square poker as an honorable occupation; for even the California legislature had legalized it as such. Jim used to praise me for some of my plays, and cussed me for a bonehead on others.

I was now constantly coming in contact with the roving gamblers of the West, that restless class of drifters who followed the boom-camp trails from the Rockies to the shore of the Pacific, and from Mexico to the interior of the British possessions on the north. They told lurid tales of fortunes won and lost, of their wild dissipations when flush with money, of gun fights, their horror of the Mexican stiletto, of the little-known lands of the states and territories; and always there was some place just ahead where they were going to clean up big on the gambling games. It was the spirit of the gold diggers itself in reality that animated them—the gold diggers, their ancestors, who had forever drifted as they panned the streams of the West in their search for gold. But the time had now come when the easily obtained virgin metal of the streams and river bars was

The thrill of uncertainty lured these men to the gambling table, their forefathers to the stream for gold.

one. I was simply out of my class, a maverick of the range, and as such it was proper that I should be slaughtered and apportioned among them.

Well, I was. The next day my diamond went in hock. Within a week my clothes had been exchanged for overalls; I was stretching wire, hauling water and cooking for a hay-baling outfit near West Lake Park. I worked from four in the morning until ten at night, and my wages were one dollar a day. I slept in a haystack with a quiet, small-built man, who confided to me that he had recently lost all his money in a poker game at San Pedro. Later on it developed that he had brutally murdered several people, and he was hung for the crime.

Times were tough those days in Los Angeles, yet whenever I secured a dollar, the eagle on it always lit in a poker game. I peddled hot tamales, sold ice cream, worked for a junkman, bought and sold oil cans, waited on table, washed dishes; and often, being out of work, was desperately hungry. However, I stolidly endured it all, and for one object only—a poker stake. Yet somehow I could never connect with a winning. So one day,

with less than a dollar in my pocket, I boarded a freight train for Yuma, Arizona. I had always heard a lot about Yuma, but I found it worse than reported. I couldn't get work for meals and the sun was so hot that it seemed to crinkle my skin. At the end of three days I was so nearly starved that I begged a meal from some Indians who were camped on the edge of the town. They fed me a sort of meat stew from an iron pot. I never knew whether it was rattlesnake, Gila monster, lizard, or just dog; but whatever it was, I never ate a better meal. I stayed at their camp that night; and the next morning, in company with a number of their inhabitants, I boarded a freight train for Tucson.

As the train slowed down before entering the town I dropped off and started walking along the railroad track. I had gone but a short distance when I noticed four fellows squatted around an oil can which was propped above a small fire.

"Hey, bo, which way?" one of them shouted.

"El Paso," I replied, knowing full well that I was expected to name some definite destination. "I just got out of Yuma; been stranded there three days."

At my words a gorilla-like fellow jumped to his feet.

"Bo, that's enough," he said as he grabbed a greasy tomato can and shook the clustered flies from its interior. Holding to the turned-back top of the can, he dipped up a steaming mess. "Throw this feed into you, kid," he said as he handed me the tin.

It had an off smell like tainted meat; but it also contained potatoes, onions and flour thickening. A stiff breeze was blowing and sand had sifted into the stew so that my teeth were constantly shutting down on the gritty substance. Yet being desperately hungry, I downed the entire mess, the silent circle interestedly watching the process.

When I had finished, the big fellow turned to his companions and confidently remarked, "The kid's been in Yuma." Evidently the stew was the third-degree test. Gorilla, as I had termed him in my mind, then turned to me and asked, "What's your stunt, kid?"

Not quite sure of the question, I hazarded the answer, "Gambler."

A roar of laughter greeted my reply.

"Where's the glad rags and the rocks?" one of them questioned.

"In hock in Los," I briefly replied.

A hobo-looking fellow who claimed to be a gambler seemed to appeal very much to their sense of humor. However, being careful businessmen in the line of their profession, they frisked me from head to foot on the chance of finding a money plant. Then they turned to kidding me about being a gambler, and I waxed grandly eloquent in defense of my qualifications as such.

It was sundown when Gorilla told me to can the chatter and, turning to his companions, said, "Say, fellers, I got a hunch the kid's lucky. There's a dollar-a-throw stud game on the main drag of this burg. Let's pool the price an' stake the kid."

We went in a body, for apparently no one trusted the others. At the entrance to the saloon they handed me the dollar with an admonition from Gorilla that if I didn't win he would choke the gizzard out of me. At the same time he clasped and unclasped his big hands, hunched his long arms and heavy shoulders up and down, drew his face into a horrible grimace and placed it close to mine and hissed, "See, bo?" Pleasant instructions indeed on short money and a long chance.

I soon found that I had landed in a framed game and a tough hangout. The dealer was a Mexican, two of the boosters were of the same nationality, and the fourth player was a half-breed Indian. My presence at least added color to the game; and knowing a little Spanish, but pretending that I did not, I picked up advantages by listening to their conversation. The dealer raked off an overly stiff percentage whenever I won a pot. Otherwise they attempted no crooked work until I had about ten dollars in front of me. Their stuff was raw, so I easily ducked it. At the end of an hour I was sixteen dollars winner and getting mighty uneasy, for they were shooting so much work at me that I knew I could not duck it all.

By this time the hobos were pretty well stewed, and

The worthy gambler played square, knew when the other guy played crooked and took him to task for it.

I was more than pleased when Gorilla whispered in my ear, "The gang's broke an' wants alkie."

So I cashed in and we split the money five ways. I bought a round of drinks, and a few drinks later skipped out the back door while two of the hobos were engaged in a fist fight. I learned the next morning that the Tucson marshal had bundled them all into a boxcar, slipped the brakie a dollar of the hobos' money and told him to dump them off at Yuma. . . .

During the next three years that I drifted the poker route I was never broke. I clung mostly to the gold and silver camps. There was a saying that all gamblers had a dumping place for their money. With most of them it was faro bank; booze, race horses and women with others; and, peculiar as it may seem, fake stock promotions caught many of these shrewd fellows. Travel, good living and prospecting got mine.

During my six years of almost constant travel by train, stage, boat, horseback, and even many times afoot, I played poker under many varying conditions—on blankets spread in the shade of trees, or on the desert sands in the scorching heat of the summer sun; in tents bitter cold or insufferably hot; on the beds in the miners' bunk houses, in cook shacks or cabins. More often, however, it was the open barroom, where drunken fights were frequent and sometimes a deck of cards was splashed with blood. However, contrary to all lurid tales of poker games, killings were of infrequent occurrence. Then, too, there were the back rooms closed shut and reeking with the smell of liquor and the air blue with the haze of tobacco smoke. There were, as well, the well-lighted and properly ventilated gambling houses of the larger cities. Also, there were the elegantly fitted rooms in the closed towns where they gave you a shot of real liquor from a polished sideboard before you sat in the game.

Big games among gamblers often developed into endurance tests, for those who could sit the longest and drink whisky with the least effects usually got the money. Corns on your person some place besides your feet were apt to develop in those days. Long hours of steady sitting, loss of sleep, irregular meals, strong stimulants, foul air and other abusive habits caused

As exciting as the game itself were the tales it evoked.

many to become drunkards or dope fiends. Pneumonia and tuberculosis claimed many. It was a hard, fast life, and most of those who persistently followed the game slipped out in their 30s. Yet to prove the exception to the rule, there was Windy Eastman, who at 76 was still stepping as lively as the young fellows, and treading the pace.

There were "lungers" in nearly every poker game; and it was in Los Angeles in 1893, if I remember correctly, that I saw one have a hemorrhage and die at the table while raking in a big pot that he had just won.

"A noble death," the gamblers said.

His winnings were sufficient to bury him decently. The boom camps of the desert countries were whirlwinds of dust and the green-lumber shacks of the snow lands were a steaming vapor. Epidemics of contagious diseases were a frequent occurrence, and in the words of the poet, "They buried them darkly at dead of night," for deaths frightened people away. Men would sleep packed thick on the floors of the saloons, just leaving a lane to the bar and the gambling tables. The morning wakening by the porter would, more often then not, find someone cold and stiff beneath the heap of human rabble.

I never knew a death to stop the turn of a card, however. I remember playing all night by the side of a dying man. He was one of us, and we were separated by a cloth partition. It was 50 miles to a doctor and a bad night. We hired a rough camp nurse, and he told us there was no hope for Tex. Pneumonia had him. I went to the side of his bed and took his hand.

"Is there anything I can do?" I asked.

He was silent a moment, then said, "Don't stop the game. I like to hear the jingle of the coin. I wish that I could play with you boys tonight."

He drifted off into a meaningless babble and at daylight was dead. Yet I never felt that we were heartless. We all donated money for those who were sick and saw that each one, gambler or miner, was decently buried. The sporting crowd were notoriously generous to the injured or sick. We cared for the sick, but the dead were dead and beyond our help, so we went on with the games. (1923)

To the Man on Trail

A Story by Jack London

"Dump it in."

"But I say, Kid, isn't that going it a little too strong? Whiskey and alcohol's bad enough; but when it comes to brandy and pepper sauce and—"

"Dump it in. Who's making this punch, anyway?" And Malemute Kid smiled benignantly through the clouds of steam. "By the time you've been in this country as long as I have, my son, and lived on rabbit tracks and salmon belly, you'll learn that Christmas comes only once per annum. And a Christmas without punch is sinking a hole to bedrock with nary a pay streak."

"Stack up on that fer a high cyard," approved Big Jim Belden, who had come down from his claim on Mazy May to spend Christmas, and who, as everyone knew, had been living the two months past on straight moose meat. "Hain't fergot the hooch weuns made on the Tanana, hev yeh?"

"Well, I guess yes. Boys, it would have done your hearts good to see that whole tribe fighting drunk— and all because of a glorious ferment of sugar and sourdough. That was before your time," Malemute Kid said as he turned to Stanley Prince, a young mining expert who had been in two years. "No white women in the country then, and Mason wanted to get married. Ruth's father was chief of the Tananas, and objected, like the rest of the tribe. Stiff? Why, I used my last pound of sugar, finest work in that line I ever did in my life. You should have seen the chase, down the river and across the portage."

"But the squaw?" asked Louis Savoy, the tall French Canadian, becoming interested; for he had heard of this wild deed when at Forty Mile the preceding winter.

Then Malemute Kid, who was a born raconteur, told the unvarnished tale of the Northland Lochinvar. More than one rough adventurer of the North felt his heartstrings draw closer and experienced vague yearnings for the sunnier pastures of the Southland, where life promised something more than a barren struggle with cold and death.

"We struck the Yukon just behind the first ice run," he concluded, "and the tribe only a quarter of an hour behind. But that saved us; for the second run broke the jam above and shut them out. When they finally got into Nuklukayet, the whole post was ready for them. And as to the forgathering, ask Father Roubeau here— he performed the ceremony."

The Jesuit took the pipe from his lips but could only express his gratification with patriarchal smiles, while Protestant and Catholic vigorously applauded.

"By gar!" ejaculated Louis Savoy, who seemed overcome by the romance of it. "*La petite* squaw; *mon* Mason *brav.* By gar!"

Then, as the first tin cups of punch went round, Bettles the Unquenchable sprang to his feet and struck up his favorite drinking song:

There's Henry Ward Beecher
And Sunday-school teachers,
All drink of the sassafras root;
But you bet all the same,
If it had its right name,
It's the juice of the forbidden fruit.
"Oh, the juice of the forbidden fruit."

roared out the bacchanalian chorus,

Oh, the juice of the forbidden fruit;
But you bet all the same,
If it had its right name,
It's the juice of the forbidden fruit.

Malemute Kid's frightful concoction did its work; the men of the camps and trails unbent in its genial

The winter wonderland of the far north is not all it seems; danger lurks, and the wise traveler proceeds with caution.

glow, and jest and song and tales of past adventure went round. Aliens from a dozen lands, they toasted each and all. It was the Englishman, Prince, who pledged "Uncle Sam, the precocious infant of the New World," the Yankee, Bettles, who drank to "The Queen, God bless her," and together, Savoy and Meyers, the German trader, clanged their cups to Alsace and Lorraine.

Then Malemute Kid arose, cup in hand, and glanced at the greased-paper window, where the frost stood full three inches thick. "A health to the man on trail this night; may his grub hold out; may his dogs keep their legs; may his matches never miss fire."

Crack! Crack! They heard the familiar music of the dog whip, the whining howl of the malemutes, and the crunch of a sled as it drew up to the cabin. Conversation languished while they waited the issue.

"An old-timer; cares for his dogs and then himself," whispered Malemute Kid to Prince as they listened to the snapping jaws and the wolfish snarls and yelps of pain. It proclaimed to their practiced ears that the stranger was beating back their dogs while he fed his own.

Then came the expected knock, sharp and confident, and the stranger entered. Dazzled by the light, he

hesitated a moment at the door, giving to all a chance for scrutiny. He was a striking personage, and a most picturesque one, in his Arctic dress of wool and fur. Standing six foot two or three, with proportionate breadth of shoulders and depth of chest, his smooth-shaven face nipped by the cold to a gleaming pink, his long lashes and eyebrows white with ice, and the ear and neck flaps of his great wolfskin cap loosely raised, he seemed, of a verity, the Frost King, just stepped in out of the night. Clasped outside his Mackinaw jacket, a beaded belt held two large Colt's revolvers and a hunting knife, while he carried, in addition to the inevitable dog whip, a smokeless rifle of the largest bore and latest pattern. As he came forward, for all his step was firm and elastic, they could see that fatigue bore heavily upon him.

An awkward silence had fallen, but his hearty "What cheer, my lads?" put them quickly at ease, and the next instant Malemute Kid and he had gripped hands. Though they had never met, each had heard of the other, and the recognition was mutual. A sweeping introduction and a mug of punch were forced upon him before he could explain his errand.

"How long since that basket sled, with three men and eight dogs, passed?" he asked.

"An even two days ahead. Are you after them?"

"Yes; my team. Run them off under my very nose, the cusses. I've gained two days on them already— pick them up on the next run."

"Reckon they'll show spunk?" asked Belden, in order to keep up the conversation, for Malemute Kid already had the coffeepot on and was busily frying bacon and moose meat.

The stranger significantly tapped his revolvers.

"When'd yeh leave Dawson?"

"Twelve o'clock."

"Last night?"—as a matter of course.

"Today."

A murmur of surprise passed round the circle. And well it might; for it was just midnight, and seventy-five miles of rough river trail was not to be sneered at for a twelve hours' run.

The talk soon became impersonal, however, harking back to the trails of childhood. As the young stranger ate of the rude fare, Malemute Kid attentively studied his face. Nor was he long in deciding that it was fair, honest, and open, and that he liked it. Still youthful, the lines had been firmly traced by toil and hardship. Though genial in conversation, and mild when at rest, the blue eyes gave promise of the hard steel-glitter which comes when called into action, especially against odds. The heavy jaw and square-cut chin demonstrated rugged pertinacity and indomitability. Nor, though the attributes of the lion were there, was there wanting the certain softness, the hint of womanliness, which bespoke the emotional nature.

"So thet's how me an' the ol' woman got spliced," said Belden, concluding the exciting tale of his courtship. " 'Here we be, Dad,' sez she. 'An' may yeh be damned,' sez he to her, an' then to me, 'Jim, yeh—yeh get outen them good duds o' yourn; I want a right peart slice o' thet forty acre plowed 'fore dinner.' An' then he turns on her an' sez, 'An' yeh, Sal; yeh sail inter them dishes.' An' then he sort o' sniffled an' kissed her. An' I was thet happy—but he seen me an' roars out, 'Yeh, Jim!' An' yeh bet I dusted fer the barn."

"Any kids waiting for you back in the States?" asked the stranger.

"Nope; Sal died 'fore any come. Thet's why I'm here." Belden abstractedly began to light his pipe, which had failed to go out, and then brightened up with, "How 'bout yerself, stranger—married man?"

For reply, he opened his watch, slipped it from the thong which served for a chain, and passed it over. Belden picked up the slush lamp, surveyed the inside of the case critically, and, swearing admiringly to himself, handed it over to Louis Savoy. With numerous "By gars!" he finally surrendered it to Prince, and they noticed that his hands trembled and his eyes took on a peculiar softness. And so it passed from horny hand to horny hand—the pasted photograph of a woman, the clinging kind that such men fancy, with a babe at the breast. Those who had not yet seen the wonder were keen with curiosity; those who had became silent and retrospective. They could face the pinch of famine, the grip of scurvy, or the quick death by field or flood; but the pictured semblance of a strange woman and child made women and children of all.

"Never have seen the youngster yet—he's a boy, she says, and two years old," said the stranger as he received the treasure back. A lingering moment he gazed upon it, then snapped the case and turned away, but not quick enough to hide the restrained rush of tears.

Malemute Kid showed him to a bunk and bade him turn in. He obliged, willingly.

"Call me at four sharp. Don't fail me," were his last words,

With resolution that commanded respect, that virtually knew no bounds, the mounty was determined to get his man.

and a moment later he was breathing in the heaviness of exhausted sleep.

"By Jove! He's a plucky chap," commented Prince. "Three hours' sleep after seventy-five miles with the dogs, and then the trail again. Who is he, Kid?"

"Jack Westondale. Been in going on three years, with nothing but the name of working like a horse, and any amount of bad luck to his credit. I never knew him, but Sitka Charley told me about him."

"It seemed hard that a man with a sweet young wife like his and a youngun' to boot should be putting in his years in this godforsaken hole, where every year counts for two on the outside."

"The trouble with him is clean grit and stubbornness. He's cleaned up twice with a stake, but he's lost it both times."

Here the conversation was broken off by an uproar from Bettles, for the effect had begun to wear away. And soon the bleak years of monotonous grub and deadening toil were being forgotten in rough merriment. Malemute Kid alone seemed unable to lose himself, and cast many an anxious look at his watch. Once he put on his mittens and beaver-skin cap, and, leaving the cabin, fell to rummaging about in the cache.

Nor could he wait

the hour designated; for he was fifteen minutes ahead of time in rousing his guest. The young giant had stiffened badly, and brisk rubbing was necessary to bring him to his feet. He tottered painfully out of the cabin, to find his dogs harnessed and everything ready for the start. The company wished him good luck and a short chase, while Father Roubeau, hurriedly blessing him, led the stampede for the cabin; and small wonder, for it is not good to face seventy-four degrees below zero with naked ears and hands.

Malemute Kid saw him to the main trail, and there, gripping his hand heartily, gave him advice.

"You'll find a hundred pounds of salmon eggs on the sled," he said. "The dogs will go as far on that as with one hundred and fifty of fish, and you can't get dog food at Pelly, as you probably expected." The stranger started, and his eyes flashed, but he did not interrupt. "You can't get an ounce of food for dog or man til you reach Five Fingers, and that's a stiff two hundred miles. Watch out for open water on the Thirty Mile River, and be sure you take the big cutoff above Laberge."

"How did you know it? Surely the news can't be ahead of me already?"

"I don't know it; and what's more, I don't want to know it. But you never owned that team you're chasing. Sitka Charley sold it to them last spring. But he sized you up to me as square once, and I believe him. I've seen your face; I like it. And I've seen—why, damn you, hit the high places for salt water and that wife of yours, and—" Here the Kid unmittened and jerked out his sack.

"No; I don't need it," and the tears froze on his cheeks as he convulsively gripped Malemute Kid's hand.

"Then don't spare the dogs; cut them out of the traces as fast as they drop; buy them and think they're cheap at ten dollars a pound. You can get them at Five Fingers, Little Salmon, and Hootalinqua. And watch out for wet feet," was his parting advice. "Keep a-traveling up to twenty-five, but if it gets below that, build a fire and change your socks."

Fifteen minutes had barely elapsed when the jingle of bells announced new arrivals. The door opened, and a mounted policeman of the Northwest Territory entered, followed by two half-breed dog drivers. Like Westondale, they were heavily armed and showed signs of fatigue. The half-breeds had been born to the trail and bore it easily; but the young policeman was badly exhausted. Still, the dogged obstinacy of his race held him to the pace he had set, and would hold him till he dropped in his tracks.

"When did Westondale pull out?" he asked. "He stopped here, didn't he?" This was supererogatory, for the tracks told their own tale too well.

Malemute Kid had caught Belden's eye, and he, scenting the wind, replied evasively, "A right peart while back."

"Come, my man; speak up," the policeman warned.

"Yeh seem to want him right smart. Hez he ben gittin' cantankerous down Dawson way?"

"Held up Harry McFarland's for forty thousand; exchanged it at the P.C. store for a check on Seattle; and who's to stop the cashing of it if we don't overtake him? When did he pull out?"

Every eye suppressed its excitement, for Malemute Kid had given the cue, and the young officer

and Babette would have to be shot before the first mile was covered; that the rest were almost as bad; and that it would be better for all hands to rest up.

"Lend me five dogs?" he asked, turning to the Kid. But the Kid shook his head.

"I'll sign a check on Captain Constantine for five thousand—here's my papers—I'm authorized to draw at my own discretion."

Again the silent refusal.

"Then I'll requisition them in the name of the Queen."

Smiling incredulously, the Kid glanced at his well-stocked arsenal, and the English-

man, realizing his impotency, turned for the door. But, because the dog drivers were still objecting, he whirled upon them fiercely, calling them women and curs. The swart face of the older half-breed flushed angrily as he drew himself up and promised in good, round terms that he would travel his leader off his legs, and would then be delighted to plant him in the snow.

The young officer—and it required his whole will—walked steadily to the door, exhibiting a freshness he did not possess. But they all knew and appreciated his proud effort; nor could he veil the twinges of agony that shot across his face. Covered with frost, the dogs were curled up in the snow, and it was almost impossible to get them to their feet. The poor brutes whined under the stinging lash, for the dog drivers were angry and cruel; nor till Babette, the leader, was cut from the traces could they break out the sled and get under way.

encountered wooden faces on every hand.

Striding over to Prince, he put the question to him. Though it hurt him, gazing into the frank, earnest face of his fellow countryman, he replied inconsequentially on the state of the trail.

Then he espied Father Roubeau, who could not lie. "A quarter of an hour ago," the priest answered; "but he had four hours' rest for himself and dogs."

"Fifteen minutes' start, and he's fresh! My God!" the poor fellow staggered back, half fainting from exhaustion and disappointment, murmuring something about the run from Dawson in ten hours and the dogs being played out.

Malemute Kid forced a mug of punch upon him; then he turned for the door, ordering the dog drivers to follow. But the warmth and promise of rest were too tempting, and they objected strenuously. The Kid was conversant with their French patois, and followed it anxiously.

They swore that the dogs were gone up; that Siwash

"A dirty scoundrel and a liar!" "By gar! Him no good!" "A thief!" "Worse than an Indian!" It was evident that they were angry—first at the way they had been deceived; and second at the outraged ethics of the Northland, where honesty, above all, was man's prime jewel. "An' we gave the cuss a hand, after knowin what he'd did." All eyes turned accusingly upon Malemute Kid, who rose from the corner where he had been making Babette comfortable, and silently emptied the bowl for a final round of punch.

"It's a cold night, boys—a bitter cold night," was the irrelevant commencement of his defense. "You've all traveled trail, and know what that stands for. Don't jump a dog when he's down. You've only heard one side. A whiter man than Jack Westondale never ate from the same pot nor stretched blanket with you or me. Last fall he gave his whole clean-up, forty thousand, to Joe Castrell, to buy in on Dominion. Today he'd be a millionaire. But while he stayed behind at Circle City, taking care of his partner with the scurvy, what does Castrell do? Goes into McFarland's, jumps the limit, and drops the whole sack. Found him dead in the snow the next day. And poor Jack laying his plans to go out this winter to his wife and the boy he's never seen. You'll notice he took exactly what his partner lost—forty thousand. Well, he's gone out; and what are you going to do about it?"

The Kid glanced round the circle of his judges, noted the softening of their faces, then raised his mug aloft. "So a health to the man on trail this night; may his grub hold out; may his dogs keep their legs; may his matches never miss fire. God prosper him; good luck go with him; and—"

"Confusion to the Mounted Police!" cried Bettles, to the crash of the empty cups.

Prey and predator, Westondale and the mounty shared a common enemy—the elements—with all other men on trail.

They Came With *the Cattle*

From the worst bad man to the best buffalo hunter, the characters of the Old West inspired countless cowboy ballads.

Why Cowboys Sing

An Essay by J. Frank Dobie

Whoo-pee-ti-yea, git along, my little dogies,
For the camp is far away.
Whoo-pee-ti-yea, and a-driving the dogies,
For Wyoming may be our new home.

That is the chorus of one of the oldest and best-known of the cowboy songs. It has come down from the vanished trail days when, foot by foot and mile by mile, herds crept their way from the coast of Texas to Kansas, to Wyoming, and even on into Canada.

The song was made to be sung and not to be printed. It was made to be sung under certain conditions. To understand it one must hear it out with cattle that are moving or bedded down, where the air smells strong of grass and cow flesh and while the singers ride slowly to the creak of saddle leather.

Imagine a late afternoon in advancing spring around 1875. Somewhere between Brownsville and the head-waters of the Missouri a herd of stock cattle is strung out for a mile. I say "stock cattle" for cows and calves and young stuff need a hundred times more nursing and watching over than beef cattle.

The leaders of the herd are walking out as if they scented water and bed-ground grazing. On either side of the lead cattle, riding slowly and carelessly, are the point men. Strung out at long intervals behind them come the swing men. Often one of these stops to let his horse snatch a mouthful of grass; now and then one pushes sharply ahead or rides toward the rear to shove in an animal that is picking its way too far out.

At the rear, or drag, of the herd come the drag men. Their job is not so easy, for they have to keep

Music that could "soothe the savage beast" was little comfort to a sore-footed dogie who needed a free ride now and then.

constantly after a few lagging crowbait cows, played-out calves and sore-footed yearlings.

One of the men has a dogie across the saddle in front of him. By dogie is meant little calf as well as motherless calf, and the term is often applied to yearlings and even to cattle in general.

The men are not hurried. They ride too far apart to talk to one another. Now and then they yell at the cattle. They pop whips—unless the boss is one of those cowmen that won't allow whips.

They sing.

The day, the herd, the outfit I have been picturing was like hundreds of other days, herds, outfits of the trail days. It is a picture of fact, not of fancy.

Of course, not all the cowboys on all the days sang. Many a waddie could no more carry a tune than he could carry a buffalo bull. Often all hands were too busy fighting and "cussin' them dad-blamed cattle" to sing. But in general the cowboys sang.

They sang sometimes for the pure joy of singing—for their own pleasure. Again they sang to the cattle—for the pleasure of the cattle.

They sang of cows and of life in the cow country, of roundups, stampedes, prairie dogs, rattlesnakes, chuck wagons, ropes, spurs and bad horses.

They sang also of bad men, Indian fights, squatters, buffalo hunters, mule skinners, prospectors and Tom Sherman's saloon in Dodge City, the cowboy capital—of the whole frontier of which they were a part.

They sang of the mothers and homes and sweethearts that softened their memories.

"Git along, my little dogies," and the herds snailed their way on, westward and northward, across an empire of range land on which there was neither fence nor furrow. It was a lonely vastness.

Cattle are not so sensitive as horses, but like horses and men, they crave companionship, and the herds seemed to steady and to travel better by the sound of song.

It was at night, though, when the cattle were restless and likely to stampede, that singing was a necessity. Then every puncher had a chance to sing out all the verses of all the songs he could recollect and a still better chance to invent and practice new ones.

Nowadays, night herding even on the largest ranches is somewhat rare, but as long as wild cattle are

held at night, on the range, in a trap, even in a pen, men will sing to them.

"Boys, we'll have to sing to 'em tonight," the boss will say if the fences are weak or the cattle thirsty.

Then all night a man or two will circle the corrals, singing and whistling. Cattle are apt to stampede at a man who rides up on them suddenly. A hand who knows his business will always approach them at night with a song or a call.

The songs meant to quiet cattle have a plaintive or crooning note. "The Night Herding Song" is as soft and slow as "Rock-a-bye, Baby."

Oh, say, little dogies, when are you goin' to lay down
And quit this forever shiftin' around?
My limbs are weary, my seat is sore;
Oh, lay down, little dogies, like you've laid before,
Lay down, little dogies, lay down.

Cattle just naturally love music, and many a herd that went up the trail snored to the tune of some cow-puncher's fiddle. I know one old Negro who used to fiddle camp-meeting tunes. Lake Porter, an old-time trail driver who now lives on the Texas border, says:

"Often I have taken my fiddle on herd at night, and while some of my companions would lead my horse around, I agitated the catguts, reeling off such old-time tunes as 'Black Jack Grove,' 'Dinah Had a Wooden Leg,' 'Shake That Wooden Leg,' 'Dolly Oh,' 'Arkansas Traveler,' 'Give the Fiddle a Dram' and 'The Unfortunate Pup.' And those old long-horned Texas steers actually enjoyed that music."

John Young, who used to lead Porter's horse, says there never was a stampede while the fiddle was going.

A peculiar form of cowboy song for quieting cattle is the yodel, the most famous of which is called "The Texas Lullaby." Many a night I have heard it when we were holding cattle or driving through brush as thick as the darkness and wanted the cattle to keep steady.

Wild cattle huddled in a thicket will be so completely soothed down with that "Texas Lullaby" that they can be eased out into an opening.

It is a weird, weird call. "Whoo, whoo, whoo-oo, who-who-who-who, oo-oo-oo-oo-oo-ooo," it seems to go, but neither type nor note can represent the long, drawn-out strains trailing off into a mysterious echo.

Primarily, then, the original use of the cowboy song was to soothe and steady cattle. For this the note of plaintiveness is most effective. But other causes have given to most cowboy songs and ballads a tone of sadness, even of dreariness.

In the first place, the cowboy was and is sentimental. He led a very solitary life. He had time for many memories. The great spaces of prairie and mountains and the winds and the stars make men remember. Memories are nearly always tinged with sadness.

Alone but not lonely, music his faithful companion.

The tales that the cowboy heard around his campfire at night or in the gay saloon where he refreshed himself from solitude were often of sudden death—death from the stampede, from drowning, from Indian attacks, from six-shooter duels.

Hence, as many of the old English and Scotch ballads tell of tragedies, so do many cowboy ballads.

One of the best-known tragic ballads is called "When Work Is Done This Fall." The ballad begins thus:

A group of jolly cowboys
Were discussing plans one day.

Then, as the tale runs, one of them began to tell of the home and mother he was soon going back to:

When the roundup is over,
And the shipment's done this fall,
I'm going home, boys,
Just to see them all.

That night this cowboy stood guard.

It was an awful dark night, boys,
And storming very hard.

In the darkness of the storm the herd stampeded and the cowboy's horse fell, fatally crushing the rider. After the run was checked the cowboys found their dying companion, and as they gathered around him, he resumed the theme of home and mother. These final words express well enough his kindly nature:

Send my wages to my mother,
All that I have earned,
For I am afraid, boys,
My last steer I have turned.
George, you take my saddle,
And, Billy, you take my bed,
And, Fred, you take my pistol
After that I am dead.
Think of me kindly, boys,
When you look upon them all,
For I'll not see my mother
When the shipment's done this fall.

Any big outfit was, and still is, likely to have in it a puncher with a turn for making verses. No visitor to an old-time cow camp was quite so welcome as a good singer. It was the boast of many a puncher that he could "sing all night and never repeat himself."

Such a fellow on his mettle and up singing to the crowd might invent verses as he went along. A good one would become a permanent part of the song for which it was made.

Many a hero—brave frontier pioneers who met untimely deaths—would have been unsung were it not for cowboy songs.

In *Songs of the Cowboys*, N. Howard Thorp says of "The Old Chisholm Trail" that "there are several thousand verses to it—the more whiskey the more verses."

Many of the cowboy songs are imitations or parodies. "Oh Bury Me Not on the Lone Prairie," now popular everywhere, came originally from an old song called "Ocean Burial."

A striking fact is that the best songs, no matter of what origin and no matter whether they are tragic, religious or humorous, are racy with the vernacular and ideas of range life. In the solemn verses of "Last Night as I Lay on the Prairie," heaven is a cattle range and God a cow boss:

They say there will be a great roundup
Where cowboys like dogies shall stand,
To be cut by the Rider of Judgment,
Who is posted and knows every brand.

The "top hand" is thus realistically sung of:

See him in town with a crowd that he knows
Rolling cigarettes an' a-smoking through his nose.
First thing he tells you, he owns a certain brand,
Leads you to think he is a daisy hand.

Buckskin Joe is described in the following:

The lions on the mountains I've
    drove them to their lairs;
The wildcats are my playmates, and I've
    wrestled grizzly bears.
I'm wild and woolly and full of fleas,
And I've never been curried
    below the knees.

A considerable number of cowboy songs deal with the lives of noted frontiersmen, such as Mustang Grey, California Joe, John Garner, Jesse James, Cole Younger, Billy the Kid and Sam Bass. The outlaws loom large in these songs. It would be hard to find anywhere a genuine cowpuncher who does not know Sam Bass.

Sam Bass was
    born in Indiana,
    that was his
    native home,
And at the age of
    seventeen young
    Sam began to roam.
He first came out to
    Texas, a cowboy for to be;
A kinder hearted feller you seldom ever see.

The facts that led up to Sam's capture by the Texas Rangers are then recounted with vivid rapidity.

Cowboy songs have probably extended over a larger area than any other class of folk songs. It is a long way from Brownsville to Butte, but many a cowhand was as familiar with the Bad Lands of Montana as with the *mesquitals* of the Rio Grande. That is why the same songs were sung all up and down the line.

They were carried from man to man and from camp to camp by word of mouth, almost never by the printed word. Now they are collected in books and it is a wonder that the versions don't differ more than they do.

No matter what their literary value—and others can pass on that—something in them makes them appeal to all the world.

The old cowboy songs and ballads are still sung. New ones are still being made.

But every year the farmer and the little ranchman take over thousands of acres from the cattle ranges. Every year the old-style cowboys and cowmen who are carrying on the traditions of the past become fewer. Every year the cowboy is brought a little closer to the phonograph, the radio, the picture show, the popular magazine—and the imitation cowboy.

As he comes closer to these agents of standardized society he comes to depend more and more on them for his amusement and less and less on his own memory and invention. Something like decay in the art of making and passing on the cowboy songs can be detected.

"Little Joe, the Wrangler," the story of another stampede tragedy, properly begins thus:

It's Little Joe, the
    Wrangler, he'll
    wrangle never
    more,
For his days with the
    remuda—they are
    done.

"Remuda" is Mexican for saddle horses. In a version of the song furnished me recently from a modern cowpuncher of the Llano country of Texas, which is still a good cattle country, the second line is somewhat different:

It's Little Joe, the Wrangler, he'll wrangle
    never more,
For his days with the movies, they are o'er.

But if the cowboy songs and ballads are beginning to be a memory as compared with their heyday in the times of open ranges and long trails, they are only beginning to be so.

For a long time yet they will thrive strong and fresh in a vast territory that only cattle and cattle folk can prosper in. (1925)

The Heraldry of the Range

An Editorial by J. Frank Dobie

If names and addresses were not so long they would be branded on cattle. A brand is a seal that stands for a name, and somewhere, with name and address, every legal brand is recorded, just as with the purchaser's name are recorded the make and engine number of every automobile, somewhere.

The range is branded with brands, and branded deep. The knowledge of brands is a special knowledge, and the language expressing that knowledge is a special language, hieroglyphic as well as utilitarian; familiarity with it stamping ranch people far more genuinely than such purchasable equipment as boots and spurs.

At a one-teacher school out in the mesquite the Friday afternoon session usually closed with recitations. A frequent recitation began with the well-known injunction to the little star:

Twinkle, twinkle, little star!
How I wonder what you are,
Up above the world so high
Like a diamond in the sky.

One of the school urchins was the son of a rancher who ran the Diamond P brand—⟨P⟩ . That was the only diamond the lad knew, and he confesses now that he used to study the stars by the hour, trying to catch one of them assuming the diamond shape so familiar to him on the sides of cows and at the hot end of a branding iron. He knew the language of brands better than he knew the language of jewels and poetry.

The brand fixes its language to everything pertaining to it. The chuck wagon on the Olmos—Elms—Ranch is seldom called the Olmos wagon, but is almost invariably referred to as the "A Dot wagon"; /A\ being the ranch brand. The cow crowd working on the Withers range is customarily referred to not as the Withers outfit but as the "Pig Pen outfit"; the Pig Pen, made thus— ⊞ being the Withers brand. A cowboy rides a "Double Circle horse," which is branded ◎ . Another cowboy is "one of the Spur hands." A herd in the distance "looks like a Long L herd."

A ranch may be named for its owner, as the Kokernot Ranch; it may be named after a creek or some other topographical unit on it, as the San Francisco Ranch; it may derive its name from some event in local history, as the Wagon Sheet Ranch, where a camper once drove off, absent-mindedly leaving his wagon sheet behind; or, as more often, a ranch may derive its name from something in nature pertaining to the place of its location, as the Seven Oaks and the Cochina—Hog. The famous Jingle-Bob outfit took its name from an earmark—the jingle-bob—a deep split that left the lower half of the ear flopping down. But the greater number of ranches by far take their names simply from the ranch brand—the J A ranch—⌐/A⌐—the Pitchfork—Ψ —the Hundred and One— |O|.

The very owner of a ranch sometimes loses his name in his brand. There was W 6 Wright of the Nueces, who considered it a great joke when he found that he had signed the bond of a man indicted for stealing yearlings—Wright's own brand. There is W6 Diamond and a Half Hud of the plains, who signs his checks as W. D. Hudson and gives 𝓟 as his brand. There is the S M S Kid, who has not been a kid for 40 years, but who is still helping to burn ᒿ∿ᒉ on white-faced calves. Colonel B. H. Campbell, a prominent cowman of the Indian Territory who for a time managed the great X I T Ranch of Texas, gave for his brand ̅B̅Q̅ . It was read as "Barbeque," and "Barbeque Campbell" has been a household word all over the Southwest for over half a century.

The average cowhand is so conscious of brands that in season and out of season, appropriately and inappropriately, consciously and unconsciously, he brands whatever he comes across. He whittles brands on sticks; he burns them into the planks of branding chutes, on pasture gates, on the anchor posts of windmill towers. He smears them with axle grease across the doors of barns and garages. He paints them with charcoal on the rock walls of canyons in which he has made a campfire. He carves them into his spur straps, leggings and saddle—above all, into his boot tops. "My pistol belt," says an old train driver, "had brands on it representing ranges from Chihuahua to Montana." More pistols were etched with cattle brands than were ever notched for dead victims. Many a cook has stenciled the ranch coat of arms into the top crust of that gala-day treat—a wild-plum cobbler. Ranch boys are incorrigible when it comes

to carving brands on their desks at school. They play ranch, and with baling wire for running irons brand oak balls, the sawed-off tips of horns, spools, and other objects used to represent cattle and horses.

Unconscious of or callous to any cruelty, cowboys will mark and brand a buck deer they have roped, a coyote, or anything else. Once, at least, some of them branded a catfish. This is the story:

Along in the early '80s Jeff Maltby and two other range men were reconnoitering in the Big Bend of Texas for the purpose of locating a new ranch. One evening they killed a fat black-tailed buck and shortly thereafter pitched camp beside the Rio Grande. They

had an abundance of meat, but even after one of them had shot a wild goose and another had hooked some nice fish, the sight of an enormous catfish flouncing in the river provoked a desire for more game. The only tackle they had was a slender fishing line and a small hook.

Jeff Maltby baited the hook and threw it in. Almost immediately the big catfish took it. He moved off and, without checking, broke the line. Maltby was determined to have that monster catfish. He chopped and trimmed one of the deer antlers until it resembled a huge fishhook. Then he baited it with about five pounds of venison, tied a stout rope to it, cast it in and staked the rope for the night. The next morning the catfish was on the rope.

He was the granddaddy of all the catfish in the Rio Grande. The men had fish already; they had a fat goose and more venison than they could carry. They really had no use for more meat.

"Boys," said Maltby, "it would be a shame to let the buzzards eat this critter. I'm going to turn him loose again in the big water, but first I'm going to slap my brand on him."

Then Maltby removed his bridle bit from

the headstall and reins, put it in the fire, heated it, and then neatly, but not deep, burned ◯—β into the side of the leviathan. When released, according to Maltby, "he swam a few feet, turned down his head, threw up his tail and disappeared beneath the waters."

An old-time, dyed-in-the-wool cowman took pride in nothing more than in his memory for brands, and good cowmen still take the same pride. There are hotel clerks who never forget a face, scholars who

Longhorns withstood the harsh climate of the Western plains more successfully than other cattle. Over 5 million were driven to market from 1866 to 1885.

never falter on a date and automobile salesmen who hold in mind the engine number of every car sold or inspected. One must marvel with Mark Twain at the memory of a trained Mississippi River steamboat pilot. But the memory of a top brand man surpasses any other kind of memory I have ever met or heard of. It is more than memory; it is an instinct for cattle. Still riding the range are men who can count a hundred head of mixed cattle as they string along, and then from memory classify them and give every brand correctly.

Deciphering and remembering the many letters, figures, curves and other configurations that make up brands is not enough. The thoroughgoing range man is a master of brand nomenclature, on the esoteric principles of which somebody ought to write a grammar. Generally, be it said, brands read from top to bottom and from left to right. Many brands—probably a majority of them—are so simple that nearly anybody can call them properly. The brand H 4 can be nothing else than H Four; H▷ will easily be conceived to be the H Triangle. But only the initiated denominate ⊥ as Lazy H, or Ƨ as Crazy Three. Any letter "too tired to stand up" is "lazy;" though if it is merely in an oblique position and not on its back, it is "tumbling." ⟨ or ⟩ is Tumbling T.

A letter with curves at the ends is often said to be "running." The most noted illustration of this principle is the Running W brand, ⌇⌇⌇ , of the $1,000,000-acre King Ranch, which, however, Mexicans call *La Viborita*—Little Snake. A letter or figure with "wings" to it is "flying"—thus, ⋁ is the "Flying W."

Brands "walk," "drag," "swing," and "rock" as well as "run" or "fly." Ƒ is the Walking F and Ɋ is the

Walking A. The projection at the bottom of the figure makes ⏋ the Drag Seven. L suspended from a curve, ⌒ L, becomes the Swinging L. Many brands are on rockers, as the Rocking H— ⌣H⌣ . But if the rocker is unjoined, then it is a half or quarter circle; so ⌣H⌣ is H Half Circle. One of the most historic brands of the West is the Rocking Chair— ⌣h⌣ .

Sometimes a brand rests on a "bench," as ⅄ , the Y Bench. V-shaped prongs attached to some part of a letter make it forked. ⤜S is Forked S, but ⫫ is not Forked N; it is Forked Lightning.

A brand bromide is of the Dutchman who met a cowboy one day. "Say," he asked, "have you seen anything of my old gray mare with a drag rope on branded Hell up and Hell down?" The cowboy had seen a mare branded ⅂L —"L up and L down."

A straight mark is usually a bar, but if it is very long or leaning at an angle to the normal horizontal position, it is apt to be called a slash, and ⊢——⊣ is Bradded Dash. The ＼／ is called Cut and Slash. John Chisum, of Jingle-Bob fame, branded 20,000 calves a year with a straight line running from shoulder to tail, a bar known all over the cattle country as the Fence Rail. A brand burner added to it thus— ——Ω—— — and the result was known both as Knot on the Rail and Bug on the Rail. The Kellog boys in the Big Bend of Texas branded N on the shoulder and K on the hip, connected with a bar, but instead of being called N Bar K, the brand is called N Chain K. O—O might be O Bar O, but it isn't. It is Hobble O, for it resembles a pair of horse hobbles.

The identical brand may go by one name in one section and by another name in another section. The great Laureles—Laurel Leaf— Ranch on the Rio Grande gave the Laurel Leaf brand, but the same insignia 300 miles north on the San Saba went under the name of Flowering Lucy—a patent corruption of flower-de-luce, itself a degeneration from *fleur-de-lis*. A flattened O may be Goose Egg, Mashed O, or Link. ▢ is both Box and Block.

One time a rancher out on the Pecos started a new brand configured thus— ⌒⌣ . Somebody asked him what he ⌒⌣ called it. "*Quien sabe?*" he replied—Who knows? And as the Quien Sabe brand it was known ever afterward. Looking through a mixed herd of cattle or a brand book, one might note many brands of apparently *quien sabe* nature, but somehow the range men have usually found a name for the most nameless device—except-ing always Mexican brands. Belden Gilpin of the border country took for his brand ⟁ . Somebody might have called it Cross Triangle, △ but a Mexican said it looked like a *muneca*—a doll—and the Muneca brand it became.

Confessedly, then, the names for a great many brand devices are purely a matter of personal interpretation. A well-known brand of Wise County, Texas, was the Gourd and Vine. It was run in this manner, ⟿⟿ so as to cover the whole side of an animal, and though everybody called it Gourd and Vine, the name was obviously arbitrary.

Some brands, because of the oddity of the device or name, became better known than certain simpler brands much more widely used. Such a brand was ⟋⟍ . Originally it was known as Pot Hooks. It was run on the Colorado River, Texas, by McAulay and Clampitt. In the drought of 1884 their herd of 10,000 cattle was reduced to 5,000, and they moved farther west into the Green Valley. Here the brand took the name of Straddle Bug. It began on the shoulder and ended at the rear of the animal's thigh. It was said: "The only way for a cow thief to burn the Straddle Bug out was to burn up the brute wearing it."

In the days of the open range, calves were roped out of the roundup and dragged to a branding fire nearby. As a cowboy dragged up a calf he called out the brand and earmark to be run on it—the mark and brand, that is, of the mother cow, which he observed as he roped the calf. The cowboys sang out these brands loud and high, and frequently indulged in variations that stuck. One brand of the Pecos country was I D A —I D A Bar. As a cowboy dragged up a calf he called out, "Ida on a rail," and the name of the brand thence-forth was Ida on a Rail.

George Evans in the Davis Mountains west of the Pecos gave K A T E, as a compliment to his wife. He got his mail at a wide place in the road called Borracho. One day at a roundup near Borracho a harum-scarum cowboy dragged a fat calf up to the fire, at the same time yelling, "Katie, my wife, Borracho, Texas." Thence-forth the K A T E brand was often called "Katie, my wife, Borracho, Texas."

Though new brands are constantly being recorded the most interesting and original belong to the past.

Just when brands were introduced to the world would be difficult to say. The claim has often

A cowboy's saddle was his most prized possession. During roundup, he might spend 60 hours straight in it.

been made that Cortes, conqueror of Mexico, originated branding not only in America but in the world. He may have branded first in America, but certainly not in the world. It is said that a tomb 2,500 years old has been uncovered in Thebes bearing among other mural decorations the representation of a cow tied down and a man branding her with a geometric design. The tomb must have been that of an Egyptian cattle king. When Chaucer's pilgrims set out on their immortal journey from London to Canterbury more than 500 years ago, some of them probably rode on rented horses. At least, horses kept for rent at that time were, says the great historian, Jusserand—who cites authority for the statement—"branded in a prominent man-

ner, so that unscrupulous travelers should not be tempted to quit the road and appropriate the steeds." Indeed, Will C. Barnes has traced branding in England back to the eighth century. In 1643, before the cattle industry in the Southwest was born, the New Haven, Connecticut, code stipulated how horses should be branded in order to prevent any trouble between rival claimants of what were called "horses running together in the woods."

A brand might spring forth full-grown without premeditation, but with most cowmen choosing a brand has always been a more serious matter than naming a baby. The practical cowman wants a brand that is plain and easily read. He wants it large enough that it cannot be blotched or run out by cow thieves, and at the same time not so large that it will ruin the value of the hide. In the old days it was more important than it is now to have a brand that does not lend itself to being run into another brand. The Straddle Bug, already described, well illustrates the fulfillment of this latter requisite. Some cowmen have preferred curves, for a square corner in a brand is often branded so deep that it becomes raw and sore, inviting blowflies and screw worms. Other cowmen have preferred straight lines and boxes. "Take a brand like ꝑ or ⊕ or $," said D. B. Gardner, manager of the Pitchfork Cattle Company. "The whole area between the lines of such a brand may be blistered by a very hot stamp iron, especially on the tender skin of young calves. The only good brand is a brand that peels with the lines."

There are legendary tales about brands, as there are about everything else with which man has had a vital connection. One of the best known of these legends tells how the Four Sixes— 6 666 —originated.

Back in the early days a young cowboy by

One of his opponents was desperate. "Burk," he said, "I'm broke, but I'll play my ranch and cattle against your pile."

"You've made a bet," was the reply.

On the deal Burk Burnett drew two sixes. He discarded three other cards, keeping the pair. Then he drew two more sixes. The four sixes won the ranch. Immediately, the story goes on, Burnett rebranded the cattle he had won with his lucky number, 6666. In time he increased his holdings until he had 300,000 acres in the Indian Territory stocked with Four Sixes cattle, besides an enormous ranch in North Texas. An oil field came in on his land and a boom city named Burkburnett sprang up. When his widow died, only a few years ago, she left several million dollars to Texas Christian University—probably the best poker hand that a Christian institution ever drew.

Tragedy has been recorded in cattle brands. At a roundup in the Big Bend country about 1890, Fine Gilleland cut a maverick

the name of Burk Burnett, who was just getting his start in cattle, rode into the village of Fort Worth one morning, bent on indulging his skill in the favorite game of the range—poker. At one of the many gaming tables, then wide open to the public, he invested in a sombrero full of chips. At first he lost heavily; then the game became variable; about midnight his luck changed, and by daylight he had a barrel full of money.

yearling out of the herd and was driving it to his bunch when a man by the name of Poe dashed up, disputing the ownership. Gilleland turned upon Poe with his six-shooter, killed him and fled. Cowboys then threw the animal of disputed ownership and in big letters branded across its ribs

MURDER. Two or three other killings can be traced to the quarrel. The yearling was well branded. According to tradition, it became an outcast from other cattle. No one wanted it. It grew gray with years and finally disappeared, presumably victim to winter blizzard.

Out in Colorado, so another tale runs, a cowboy by the name of Jess Hitson failed to come in one night. This was in July, 1868. For three years his disappearance was a mystery. Then one day a steer was found bearing this brand: The 7-4-68 INDIANS HOT AS HELL JH brand told the story of how Jess Hitson was branding a maverick when he saw Indians coming. He took time to write his fate before he met it. The savages who got him let the branded messenger go.

No account of brands would be complete without consideration of the art of burning out brands. It was an art that reached the height of development during the days of open range, but it is by no means lost yet. Before the practice of counterbranding went out, a thief might void a brand by running a bar through it or by counterbranding the animal—as if it had been legitimately sold—and then putting his own brand on it. Again, he might rub out the owner's brand by taking a hot smoothing iron and burning all that part of an animal's hide covered by a brand. This was called blotching, or blotting. The result would be an enormous scar or blotch, through which the original lines were apt still to be visible. In any case, the blotch was evidence that the animal had been stolen, though not always could it be ascertained from whom stolen.

The most common practice by far was, and is yet, to change the original brand into something different.

Although brand burning forms a lurid and picturesque feature in the history of the range, its extent has often been overemphasized. After all, a great majority of range men were honest, and the brands on cattle, as a general rule, served the purpose for which they have always been designed—that is, to identify and maintain ownership.

When all the stories about picturesque brands have been told, the fact remains that the great majority of brands are not picturesque. They are a part of a great industry, and in every state where the grazing industry obtains they are to be found recorded in ponderous legal tomes, listed first under the letters of the alphabet, then under numbers from one to ten, and then under symbols.

If branding could be avoided, it would be avoided. Humane societies have protested against the practice; experiments have been conducted with chemical compositions purporting to make an indelible but painless mark. But no substitute has been found for branding. Anyhow, branding is not unduly cruel and the resultant pain is of short duration. As long as there are ranches, there will be brands. The heraldry of the range is not obsolete; it is not even obsolescent.

Cutting calves from the herd and noting the brand of the mother cow were the first steps in the branding process which served a dual purpose: to identify and maintain ownership and to prevent rustling.

The Bride Comes to Yellow Sky

A Story by Stephen Crane

The great Pullman was whirling onward with such dignity of motion that a glance from the window seemed simply to prove that the plains of Texas were pouring eastward. Vast flats of green grass, dull-hued spaces of mesquite and cactus, little groups of frame houses, woods of light and tender trees, all were sweeping into the east, sweeping over the horizon, a precipice.

A newly married pair had boarded this coach at San Antonio. The man's face was reddened from many days in the wind and sun, and a direct result of his new black clothes was that his brick-colored hands were constantly performing in a most conscious fashion. From time to time he looked down respectfully at his attire. He sat with a hand on each knee, like a man waiting in a barber's shop. The glances he devoted to other passengers were furtive and shy.

The bride was not pretty, nor was she very young. She wore a dress of blue cashmere, with small reservations of velvet here and there, and with steel buttons abounding. She continually twisted her head to regard her puff sleeves, very stiff, straight and high. They embarrassed her. It was quite apparent that she had cooked, and that she expected to cook, dutifully. The blushes caused by the careless scrutiny of some passengers as she had entered the car were strange to see upon this plain, underclass countenance, which was drawn in placid, almost emotionless lines.

They were evidently very happy. "Ever been in a parlor-car before?" he asked, smiling with delight.

"No," she answered; "I never was. It's fine, though, ain't it?"

"Great! And then after a while we'll go forward to the diner, and get a big lay-out. Finest meal in the world. Charge a dollar."

"Charge a dollar?" cried the bride. "Why, that's too much —for us—ain't it, Jack?"

"Not this trip, anyhow," he answered bravely. "We're going to go the whole thing."

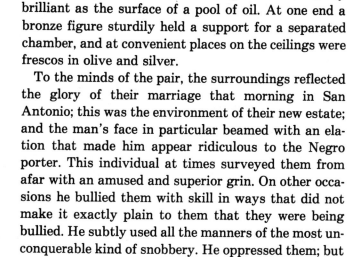

Later he explained to her about the trains. "You see, it's a thousand miles from one end of Texas to the other; and this train runs right across it, and never stops but four times." He had the pride of an owner. He pointed out to her the dazzling fittings of the coach; and in truth her eyes opened wider as she contemplated the sea-green figured velvet, the shining brass, silver and glass, the wood that gleamed as darkly brilliant as the surface of a pool of oil. At one end a bronze figure sturdily held a support for a separated chamber, and at convenient places on the ceilings were frescos in olive and silver.

To the minds of the pair, the surroundings reflected the glory of their marriage that morning in San Antonio; this was the environment of their new estate; and the man's face in particular beamed with an elation that made him appear ridiculous to the Negro porter. This individual at times surveyed them from afar with an amused and superior grin. On other occasions he bullied them with skill in ways that did not make it exactly plain to them that they were being bullied. He subtly used all the manners of the most unconquerable kind of snobbery. He oppressed them; but of this oppression they had small knowledge, and they speedily forgot that infrequently a number of travelers covered them with stares of derisive enjoyment. Historically there was supposed to be something infinitely humorous in their situation.

"We are due in Yellow Sky at 3:42," he said, looking tenderly into her eyes.

"Oh, are we?" she said, as if she had not been aware of it. To evince surprise at her husband's statement was part of her wifely amiability. She took from a pocket a little silver watch; and as she held it before her, and stared at it with a frown of attention, the new husband's face shone.

"I bought it in San Anton' from a friend of mine," he told her gleefully.

"It's seventeen minutes

Travel in a Pullman, though cramped and dusty, could be a pleasant diversion from the monotony of the scenery.

past twelve," she said, looking up at him with a kind of shy and clumsy coquetry. A passenger, noting this play, grew excessively sardonic and winked at himself in one of the numerous mirrors.

At last they went to the dining-car. Two rows of Negro waiters, in glowing white suits, surveyed their entrance with interest, and also the equanimity, of men who had been forewarned. The pair fell to the lot of a waiter who happened to feel pleasure in steering them through their meal. He viewed them with the manner of a fatherly pilot, his countenance radiant with benevolence. The patronage, entwined with the ordi-

nary deference, was not plain to them. And yet, as they returned to their coach, they showed in their faces a sense of escape.

To the left, miles down a long purple slope, was a little ribbon of mist where moved the keening Rio Grande. The train was approaching it at an angle, and the apex was Yellow Sky. Presently it was apparent that, as the distance from Yellow Sky grew shorter, the husband became commensurately restless. His brick-red hands were more insistent in their prominence. Occasionally he was rather absent-minded and far-away when the bride leaned forward and addressed him.

As a matter of fact, Jack Potter was beginning to find the shadow of a deed weigh upon him like a leaden slab. He, the town marshal of Yellow Sky, a man known, liked and feared in his corner, a prominent person, had gone to San Antonio to meet a girl he believed he loved, and there, after the usual prayers, had actually induced her to marry him, without consulting Yellow Sky for any part of the transaction. He was now bringing his bride before an innocent and unsuspecting community.

Of course, people in Yellow Sky married as it pleased them, in accordance with a general custom; but such was Potter's thought of his duty to his friends, or of their idea of his duty, or of an unspoken form which does not control men in these matters, that he felt he was heinous. He had committed an extraordinary crime. Face to face with this girl in San Antonio, and spurred by his sharp impulse, he had gone headlong over all the social hedges. At San Antonio he was like a man hidden in the dark. A knife to sever any friendly duty, any form, was easy to his hand in that remote city. But the hour of Yellow Sky was approaching.

He knew full well that his marriage was an important thing to his town. It could only be exceeded by the burning of the new hotel. His friends could not forgive him. Frequently he had reflected on the advisability of telling them by telegraph, but a new cowardice had been upon him. He feared to do it. And now the train was hurrying him toward a scene of amazement, glee and reproach. He glanced out of the window at the line of haze swinging slowly in toward the train.

Yellow Sky had a kind brass band, which played painfully, to the delight of the populace. He laughed without heart as he thought of it. If the citizens could dream of his prospective arrival with his bride, they would parade the band at the station and escort them, amid cheers and laughing congratulations, to his adobe home.

He resolved that he would use all the devices of speed and plainscraft in making the journey from the station to his house. Once within that safe citadel, he could issue some sort of vocal bulletin, and then not go among the citizens until they had time to wear off a little of their enthusiasm.

The bride looked anxiously at him. "What's worrying you, Jack?"

He laughed again. "I'm not worrying, girl; I'm only thinking of Yellow Sky."

She flushed in comprehension.

A sense of mutual guilt invaded their minds and developed a finer tenderness. They looked at each other with eyes softly aglow. But Potter often laughed the same nervous laugh; the flush upon the bride's face seemed quite permanent.

The traitor to the feelings of Yellow Sky narrowly watched the speeding landscape. "We're nearly there," he said.

Presently the porter came and announced the proximity of Potter's home. He held a brush in his hand, and, with all his airy superiority gone, he brushed Potter's new clothes as the latter slowly turned this way and that way. Potter fumbled out a coin and gave it to the porter, as he had seen others do. It was a heavy and muscle-bound business, as that of a man shoeing his first horse.

The porter took their bag, and as the train began to slow they moved forward to the hooded platform of the car. Presently the two engines and their long string of coaches rushed into the station of Yellow Sky.

"They have to take water here," said Potter, from a constricted throat and in mournful cadence, as one announcing death. Before the train stopped, his eye had swept the length of the platform, and he was glad and astonished to see there was none upon it but the station-agent, who, with a slightly hurried and anxious air, was walking toward the water-tanks. When the train had halted, the porter alighted first, and placed in position a little temporary step.

"Come on, girl," said Potter, hoarsely. As he helped her down they each laughed on a false note. He took the bag from the Negro, and bade his wife cling to his arm. As they slunk rapidly away, his hang-dog glance perceived that they were unloading the two trunks, and also that the station-agent, far ahead near the

Tavern and store owners relied upon watchdogs to alert them to visitors or any surreptitious activities.

baggage-car, had turned and was running toward him, making gestures. He laughed, and groaned as he laughed, when he noted the first effect of his marital bliss upon Yellow Sky. He gripped his wife's arm firmly to his side, and they fled. Behind them the porter stood, chuckling fatuously.

The California express on the Southern Railway was due at Yellow Sky in twenty-one minutes. There were six men at the bar of the Weary Gentleman saloon. One was a drummer who talked a great deal and rapidly; three were Texans who did not care to talk at that time; and two were Mexican sheepherders, who did not talk as a general practice in the Weary Gentleman saloon. The barkeeper's dog lay on the board walk that crossed in front of the door. His head was on his paws, and he glanced drowsily here and there with the constant vigilance of a dog that is kicked on occasion. Across the sandy street were some vivid green grass-plots, so wonderful in appearance, amid the sands that burned near them in a blazing sun, that they caused a doubt in the mind. They exactly resembled the grass mats used to represent lawns on the stage. At the cooler end of the railway station, a man without a coat sat in a tilted chair and smoked his pipe. The fresh-cut bank of the Rio Grande circled near the town, and there could be seen beyond it a great plum-colored plain of mesquite.

Save for the busy drummer and his companions in

the saloon, Yellow Sky was dozing. The newcomer leaned gracefully upon the bar, and recited with the confidence of a bard who has come upon a new field.

"—and at the same moment that the old man fell down the stairs with the bureau in his arms, the old woman was coming up with two scuttles of coal, and of course—"

The drummer's tale was interrupted by a young man who suddenly appeared in the open door. He cried: "Scratchy Wilson's drunk and has turned loose with boths hands." The two Mexicans at once set down their glasses and faded out of the rear entrance of the saloon.

The drummer, innocent and jocular, answered: "All right, old man. S'pose he has? Come in and have a drink, anyhow."

But the information had made such an obvious cleft in every skull in the room that the drummer was obliged to see its importance. All had become instantly solemn. "Say," said he, mystified, "what is this?" His three companions made the introductory gesture of eloquent speech; but the young man at the door forestalled them.

"It means, my friend," he answered, as he came into the saloon, "that for the next two hours this town won't be a health resort."

The barkeeper went to the door, and locked and barred it securely; reaching out of the window, he pulled in the heavy wooden shutters and barred them as well. Immediately a solemn, chapel-like gloom descended upon the place. The drummer was looking anxiously from one to the other.

"But say," he cried, "what is this, anyhow? You don't mean there is going to be a gun-fight?"

"Don't know whether there'll be a fight or not," answered one man, grimly; "but there'll be some shootin'—some good shootin'."

The young man who had warned them waved his hand. "Oh, there'll be a fight fast enough, if anyone wants it. Anybody can get a fight out there in the street. There's a fight just waiting."

The drummer seemed to

be swayed between the interest of a foreigner and a perception of personal danger.

"What did you say his name was?" he asked.

"Scratchy Wilson," they answered in chorus.

"And will he kill anybody? What are you going to do? Does this happen often? Does he rampage around like this once a week or so? Can he break in that door?"

"No; he can't break down that door," replied the barkeeper. "He's tried it three times. But when he comes you'd better lay down on the floor, stranger. He's dead sure to shoot at it, and a bullet may come through."

A cowboy known for his reputation as a "fast gun" was accorded respect and solitude by the townspeople.

"You better come with me back of the bar."

"No, thanks," said the drummer, perspiring; "I'd rather be where I can make a break for the back door."

Whereupon the man of bottles made a kindly but peremptory gesture. The drummer obeyed it, and, finding himself seated on a box with his head below the level of the bar, balm was laid upon his soul at sight of various zinc and copper fittings that bore a resemblance to armor-plate. The barkeeper took a seat comfortably upon an adjacent box.

"You see," he whispered, "this here Scratchy Wilson is a wonder with a gun—a perfect wonder; and when he goes on the war-trail, we hunt our holes—naturally. He's about the last one of the old gang that used to hang out along the river here. He's a terror when he's drunk. When he's sober he's all right—kind of simple—wouldn't hurt a fly—nicest fellow in town. But when he's drunk—whoo!"

The voices had toned away to mere whisperings. The drummer wished to ask more questions, which were born of an increasing anxiety and bewilderment; but when he attempted them, the men merely looked at him in irritation and motioned him to remain silent. A tense waiting hush was upon them. In the deep shadows of the room their eyes shone as they listened for sounds from the street. One man made three gestures at the barkeeper; and the latter, moving like a ghost, handed him a glass and a bottle. The man poured a full glass of whiskey, and set down the bottle noiselessly. He gulped the whiskey in a swallow, and turned again toward the door in immovable silence. The drummer saw that the barkeeper, without a sound, had taken a Winchester from beneath the bar. Later he saw this individual beckoning to him, so he tiptoed across the room.

Thereafter the drummer kept a strict eye upon the door. The time had not yet been called for him to hug the floor, but, as a minor precaution, he sidled near to the wall. "Will he kill anybody?" he said again.

The men laughed low and scornfully at the question.

"He's out to shoot, and he's out for trouble. Don't see any good in experimentin' with him."

"But what do you do in a case like this? What do you do?"

A man responded: "Why, he and Jack Potter—"

"But," in chorus the other men interrupted, "Jack Potter's in San Anton'."

"Well, who is he? What's he got to do with it?"

"Oh, he's the town marshal. He goes out and fights Scratchy when he gets on one of these tears."

"Wow!" said the drummer, mopping his brow. "Nice job he's got."

There were periods of stillness. "I wish Jack Potter was back from San Anton'," said the barkeeper. "He shot Wilson up once in the leg—and he would sail in

and pull out the kinks in this

Presently they heard a distance the sound of a shot, followed by three wild yowls. It instantly removed a bond from the men in the darkened saloon. There was a shuttling of feet. They looked at each other. "Here he comes," they said.

A man in a maroon-colored shirt, which had been purchased for purposes

thing."

from

of decoration, and made principally by some Jewish women on the East Side of New York, rounded a corner and walked into the middle of the main street of Yellow Sky.

In either hand the man held a long, blue-black revolver. Often he yelled, and these cries sang through a semblance of a deserted village, shrilly flying over roofs in a volume that seemed to have no relation to the ordinary vocal strength of a man. It was as if the surrounding stillness formed the arch of a tomb over him. These cries of ferocious challenge rang against the walls of silence. And his boots had red tops with gilded imprints, of the kind beloved in winter by little sledding boys on the hillsides of New England.

The man's face flamed in a rage begot of whiskey. His eyes, rolling, and yet keen for ambush, hunted the still doorways and windows. He walked with the creeping movement of the midnight cat. As it occurred to him, he roared menacing information. The long revolvers in his hands were as easy as straws; they were moved with an electric swiftness. The little fingers of each hand played sometimes in a musician's way. Plain from the low collar of the shirt, the cords of his neck straightened and sank, as passion moved him.

The only sounds were his terrible invitations. The calm adobes preserved their demeanor at the passing of this small thing in the middle of the deserted main street.

There was no offer of fight—no offer of fight. The man called to the sky. There were no attractions. He bellowed and fumed and swayed his revolvers here and everywhere.

The dog of the barkeeper of the Weary Gentleman saloon had not appreciated the advance of events. He yet lay dozing in front of his master's door. At sight of the dog, the man paused and raised his

Looking down the single barrel of a Colt .45 could change a viewpoint faster than any other means of persuasion.

The cowboy, though not meticulous, was very particular about his boots; despised thick-soled shoes of the East.

revolver humorously. At sight of the man, the dog sprang up and walked diagonally away, with a sullen head, and growling. The man yelled, and the dog broke into a gallop. As it was about to enter an alley, there was a loud noise, a whistling, and something spat the ground directly before it. The dog screamed, and, wheeling in terror, galloped headlong in a new direction. Again there was a noise, a whistling, and sand was kicked viciously before it. Fear-stricken, the dog turned and flurried like an animal in a pen. The man stood laughing, his weapons at his hips. Whimpering, the dog disappeared into the alley.

Ultimately, the man was attracted by the closed door of the Weary Gentleman saloon. He went to it and, hammering with a revolver, demanded drink.

The door remaining imperturbable, he picked a bit of paper from the walk, and nailed it to the framework with a knife. He then turned his back contemptuously upon this popular resort and, walking to the opposite side of the street and spinning there on his heel quickly and lithely, fired at the bit of paper. He missed it by half an inch or so. He swore at himself, and went away. Later he comfortably fusilladed the windows of his most intimate friend. The drunken man was playing with this town; it was a toy for him.

But still there was no offer of fight, no invitation. The name of Jack Potter, his ancient antagonist, entered his mind, and he concluded that it would be a glad thing if he should go to Potter's house, and by bombardment induce him to come out and fight. He moved in the direction of his desire, chanting Apache scalp-music. When he arrived at it, Potter's house presented the same still front as had the other adobes. Taking up a strategic position, the man howled a challenge. But this house regarded him as might a great stone god. It gave no sign. After a decent wait, the man howled further challenges, mingling with them curses and wonderful epithets in rapid succession.

Presently there came the spectacle of a man churning himself into deepest rage over the immobility of a house. He fumed at it as the winter wind attacks a prairie cabin in the North. As necessity bade him, he paused for breath or to reload his revolvers.

Potter and his bride walked sheepishly and with speed. Sometimes they laughed together shamefacedly.

"Next corner, dear," he said finally.

They put forth the efforts of a pair walking bowed against a strong wind. Potter was about to raise a finger to point the first appearance of the new home when, as they circled the corner, they came face to face with a man in a maroon-colored shirt, who was feverishly pushing cartridges into a large revolver. Upon the instant the man dropped his revolver to the ground and whipped another from its holster. The second weapon was aimed at the bridegroom's chest.

There was a silence. Potter's mouth seemed to be merely a grave for his tongue. He exhibited an instinct to at once loosen his arm from the woman's grip, and he dropped the bag to the sand. As for the bride, her face had gone yellow as old cloth. She was a slave to hideous rites, gazing at the apparitional snake.

The two men faced each other at a distance of three paces. He of the revolver smiled with a new and quiet ferocity.

"Tried to sneak up on me," he said. "Tried to sneak up on me!" His eyes grew more baleful. As Potter made a slight movement, the man thrust his revolver venomously forward. "No; don't you do it, Jack Potter. Don't you move a finger toward a gun just yet. Don't you move an eyelash. The time has come for me to settle with you, and I'm goin' to do it my own way, and loaf along with no interferin'. So if you don't want a gun bent on you, just mind what I tell you."

Potter looked at his enemy. "I ain't got a gun on me, Scratchy," he said. "Honest, I ain't." He was stiffening and steadying, but yet somewhere at the back of his mind a vision of the Pullman floated: the sea-green figured velvet, the shining brass, silver and glass, the wood that gleamed as darkly brilliant as the surface of a pool of oil—all the glory of the marriage, the environment of the new estate. "You know I fight when it comes to fighting, Scratchy Wilson; but I ain't got a gun on me. You'll have to do all the shootin' yourself."

His enemy's face went livid. He stepped forward, and lashed his weapon to and fro before Potter's chest. "Don't you tell me you ain't got no gun on you, you whelp. Don't tell me no lie like that. There ain't a man in Texas ever seen you without no gun. Don't take me for no kid." His eyes blazed with light, and his throat worked like a pump.

"I ain't takin' you for no kid," answered Potter. His heels had not moved an inch backward. "I'm takin' you for a damn fool. I tell you I ain't got a gun, and I ain't. If you're goin' to shoot me up, you better begin now; you'll never get a chance like this again."

So much enforced reasoning had told on Wilson's rage; he was calmer. "If you ain't got a gun, why ain't you got a gun?" he sneered. "Been to Sunday-school?"

"I ain't got a gun because I've just come from San Anton' with my wife. I'm married," said Potter. "And if I'd thought there was going to be any galoots like you prowling around when I brought my wife home, I'd had a gun, and don't you forget it."

"Married?" said Scratchy, not at all comprehending.

"Yes, married. I'm married," said Potter, distinctly.

"Married!" said Scratchy. Seemingly for the first time he saw the drooping, drowning woman at the other man's side. "No!" he said. He was like a creature allowed a glimpse of another world. He moved a pace backward, and his arm, with the revolver, dropped to his side. "Is this the lady?" he asked.

"Yes; this is the lady," answered Potter.

There was another period of silence.

"Well," said Wilson at last, slowly, "I s'pose it's all off now."

"It's all off if you say so, Scratchy. You know I didn't make the trouble." Potter lifted his valise.

"Well, I 'low it's off, Jack," said Wilson. He was looking at the ground. "Married!" He was not a student of chivalry; it was merely that in the presence of this foreign condition he was a simple child of the plains. He picked up his starboard revolver, and, placing both weapons in their holsters, he went away. His feet made funnel-shaped tracks in the sand.

The West Was
All They Knew

Tracks West

An Actual Account by Donald Culross Peattie

When I was a small boy, I thought there was no other boy whose system so much required that he ride on trains. Once I had put my lips to the smoky intoxication of travel by rail, I was a slave to it for life. I felt the craving in my bed at night, when I lay hearing the long whistle of the B. & O. going places. Early I could recite the list of the converging railroads that head into Chicago, and I could have told you where each one led away.

I would begin with the Pere Marquette, which took me to grandfather's, over in Michigan, and box the compass right around, through the Grand Trunk, the Lake Shore, the Big Four, the Nickel Plate, the Monon, the Wabash, the Rock Island, the Burlington, the Santa Fe, the Great Western, the Union Pacific, the Milwaukee-St. Paul and the Soo Line. Standing chest-deep in prairie dock and mullein along the embankment, I would watch the lengthy rumbling dragon of the freights roll past, blazoned with these names and even stranger ones—the Boston and Maine, the Central of Georgia, the Lackawanna, the Missouri Pacific—till it wagged its caboose tail at me and vanished into the sunset.

It wasn't just that I liked the lickety-split and the

toot and bustle of train travel. Even then I perceived that the shining rails probe into the heart of our continent and bring forth its secrets. As I schemed and dreamed of trains taking me to all of America, they brought to me hints of the part I longed for most, the greatest, the Western part. Into our station would come laboring a big black locomotive hoary with the ice of a blizzard encountered far out on the Nebraska prairies, so that I shivered with that distant cold. On blistering summer days, I heard the bellowing of cattle penned in their cars, and I thought I could smell the dust of the Texas panhandle, and see the cowboys riding by, easy as kings in the saddle.

I haven't changed. The biggest day in every year is the day when I wake up out on the sagebrush plains, in a westbound train, and begin to watch for the Rockies to show their white-feathered war bonnets over the rim of the world. In the observation car, I take the end chair, and sit spellbound, watching the endlessly converging and dwindling rails. That is our past which we are forever leaving. And, as I longed once for all wide America, so I yearn backward now to the boundless, unwritten, unconquered America that the searching rails found out.

I met, the other day, an old woman who had been present at the driving of the Golden Spike—a little girl then in a wide hat, trying to peep between the grown-ups; she, and most people, think that the great moment in the railroad story is that conclusive one. But in our beginnings lies all our future greatness at its purest. I choose, in railroad history, the year 1853, when the Government authorized, under the direction of the Honorable the Secretary of War, Mr. Jefferson Davis, six surveys "to ascertain," in the words of the Thirty-third Congress, "the most practicable and economical route for a railroad from the Mississippi River to the Pacific Ocean." Obedient, six expeditions started forth, from the Canadian border to the Mexican, hunting a way, through passes, over canyons, across deserts, among Apaches, Blackfeet, Paiutes, Shoshonis, for a young nation to build a one-track line—that's all we could see then, all we could afford—to link our old shores with our new.

Where they went we have doubled-tracked now. The Great Northern, the Northern Pacific, the Union Pacific, the Santa Fe, the Southern Pacific—they are all there because of a few bands of men—soldiers, surveyors, engineers, map makers. Among these useful members went a sprinkling of scientists, odd birds, boldly flying ahead of the culture they represented—geologists to help the engineers and look for signs of mineral wealth, naturalists to collect the animals, living or fossil, botanists to hunt for timber for the ties that would be laid, and to pick up by the way all the fresh and pungent things growing which had never before been adequately noted or appreciated.

Now what these expeditions did and saw is all recorded in a dozen volumes, bound in quarto as the Pacific Railway Reports. They are a collector's item with lovers of Westerniana; you pick them up, an odd volume at a time, in dusty bookshops. They are dry as the desert itself, unless you search between the lines. . . .

(One of the Scientists sent West with a railroad survey party was 21-year-old Caleb Winthrop, later a distinguished professor of botany at Harvard. The following account of an incident that took place along the way is based on the official record and on stories Winthrop told to Harvard students in later years.)

Vincente was the first to pick up Indian sign. It was a big party, he said, plenty horses, and women's moccasin prints pressed deep with the weight of the burden baskets. Then the dragoons' horses caught the smell of the Indian mounts and began to whinny and fret. The Texans sat even straighter in their saddles, drawing a shorter rein. Captain Demerrit leaned forward in the saddle, touched his mare to a trot and gained the head of the column in silence. Young Mr. Winthrop, student of the author of Hiawatha, nourished on The Last of the Mohicans, said to old Doctor Marceau, who rode at his side, "Comanches, do you think they'll be? I hope the soldiers won't want to get rough with them."

"No fear," said the surgeon dryly. "Our orders are to

Looking ahead: the surveyor, at the lay of the land; the Government, to the future of the United States.

enlist the cooperation of all the tribes. You forget, in your posy-picking, we're surveying for a railroad. Trouble is just what we don't want."

Then ahead, on a rise, they saw the wigwam village. Abruptly a dry arroyo brought them all to a halt, and down the opposite slope came riding a band of Kiowas, their lance points all akimbo, bristling and glistering in the sun, their feather bonnets tossing restless as thunderbirds, their mounts, checked by a hard bridle at the draw's edge, nickering and striking at the air with their forelegs. The voices of the women running among the wigwams came like the crying of a wild gaggle of fowl, above the hoarse raven voices of the braves.

"Mr. Winthrop," floated back the captain's cool tone, "will you have the goodness to order our interpreter forward with a flag of truce?"

Caleb, his heart thumping, interpreted this into Spanish; Doctor Marceau leaned forward from his saddle, offering a clean handkerchief; Vincente fixed it to a proffered ramrod and rode forward, the sign of amity fluttering above him, dove-white in the wind.

All the Kiowas seemed to comprehend the international symbol at once. The braves, the women, even the raving curs, fell as suddenly silent as frogs when a stone is flung in their swamp. The survey party watched tensely as the half-breed faced the full-bloods and began to pound out and point and flicker the sign

W.H.D. Koerner (1878-1938)

language common to the Indian tribes of the Plains.

Riding back at the quick trot of success, he spoke to Winthrop in his Mexican Spanish, and the young scientist, in the accents of Boston, reported to the captain that the Indians did not wish to fight; that they hoped the soldiers would not use their guns and that the whites might show their friendliness by camping in the village.

All this Demerrit accepted in a nod; he gave the command of "Forward!" and the little troop, followed by the lowing Arkansas cattle, dustily crossed this Western Rubicon.

"Indians are terrible enemies," Doctor Marceau observed to Caleb, while the Kiowas dashed, laughing and whooping, among the jostled survey party, "but so are they terrible friends."

Caleb hardly heard him. Nothing in Cooper's romances had readied him for the splendor of these fierce children of the desert. There was little red to be seen about them, save a gleam of naked thighs above the leather leggings bound with silver buckles and the streak of vermilion grease down the parting of the hair. Their faces were painted yellow; the red, white and blue feathers of their bonnets trailed in queues to the horses' flanks. Flat bands of Mexican silver bound their bare arms, and great hoops of brass swung from their ears. Their bows were studded with nails of brass and silver, and the arrows lisped and rattled in the quivers of white wolfskin. This, this, exulted Caleb, was the ultimate in primitive glory, the culminating species in the fauna of aboriginal America!

As the party entered the village, he saw for the first time in his life women bare above the girdle, and scientifically noted that no sensual admiration crossed his mind, only a pride in their proud bronze freedom. He bravely disregarded the sunny stench of the greased bodies, the kicks at which the milling curs bared needle fangs, the aspen pole, guarded by a screeching hag, from which three scalps mingled their black hairs helplessly in the wind.

A surge of respect, almost of awe, uplifted him as he glimpsed, beyond Captain Demerrit, the advancing figure of the chief—a man so splendid in his own bodily right that he seemed to disdain the trappings of his warriors. Blue-beaded moccasins and a white twist of cloth about the thighs were all his clothing; in his hand he held a pipe of red steatite with carved and feathered stem, and on a silver chain a great cross of silver glittered with his breathing against his naked chest. Facing him, the captain looked slight, thought Caleb. What were they all doing here, anyway, he demanded of himself in sudden anger—invading with the hideous threat of "progress" this self-sufficient kingdom of the free?

As the chief began to speak in slow, deep Kiowa, all

For Caleb Winthrop, seeing the native Americans in their full regalia was believing in all that he had read about them.

that Caleb had ever read in Schoolcraft's *Indian Tribes* told him what must be meant by this native oratory—the moving grandeur, the stately welcome, of what Caleb had been taught to call "the vanishing red man." He was like the orb—it came emotionally to Caleb—of some full-bodied sun going down in cloudless splendor, touching and illuminating the horizon. And then, behind the shoulder of the chief, Caleb, unbelieving, saw emerge the slim crescent of a white woman, with tragic blue eyes and a torrent of auburn hair. With one hand she held the hand of a three-year-old boy, with the other she covered her breast.

The woman, the chief, the captain, Vincente talking to the big Kiowa with his hands, the handsome child—they are all there, in Executive Document No. 91, printed by order of the House of Representatives. The item is set down with the tight-lipped, dry-eyed compassion of Captain Demerrit. For men of action do not record their emotions for print; they put down only data, dry as that pressed specimen of gilia. But is there one of us not wistful, when we dwell upon such traces of the past, for the living light, the singing blood, the heat of that long-gone day? History, really, is what you choose to make of the facts, and I am choosing, by your leave, to read between, as well as straight along, the lines of this Pacific Railway Report.

There I perceive how little Caleb Winthrop—the future Doctor Winthrop, Linnaean professor of botany at Harvard College—knew, at twenty-one, about women. He had a mother whom he took so for granted he never saw her as anything else. He had a girl, like any Harvard student, to meet in the dusk under Brattle Street lilacs. He was wholly unprepared for the woman who stepped that night out of the shadow of the cottonwoods as he walked by them toward the tent he shared with the doctor.

It was in rapid Spanish that she talked to him there in the dark, and as he listened, horror growing, he was remembering her captive beauty in sunlight, that he had watched all during the powwow. So shaken had he been by the sight that he feared it might have been through lapses of his, as translator between Vincente and the captain, that the negotiations with the Kiowa chief had gone so badly, had ended on a note of hostility. For he had been half lost in the woman's pleading gaze, so that suddenly the chief noticed this and ordered her away.

To the young New Englander, who never before had seen a woman obey a man with a look of fear, black depths opened, and when he looked up again at the

Taken prisoner in the "kingdom of the free" years ago, the woman confided all to Caleb and begged his help.

reaching her home." That could only be managed, she passionately urged upon Caleb, by her purchase from the chief, and she admitted, since he already was suspicious and angered with the whites, that the price would be great. When Caleb, in his shy young way, was kind, she flung herself upon him, sobbing.

Now were the far cool planetary principles of Caleb's life sent reeling down his darkened heavens. With hot blood, with borrowed shames and angers burning in him, he sought out Captain Demerrit. The captain, said a sentry, abruptly barring his way, was not to be disturbed. This was the hour at which he took his nightly observations on the stars.

On the gravestone of Gen. Stephen Demerrit, in the Soldiers' National Cemetery at Gettysburg, are carved the lines he loved best in life: "The starry heavens above me, the sense of duty within me." So you may guess what he said to young Caleb Winthrop, when at last he stepped back from his preoccupation with Ursa Minor and listened to the young man's furious story.

"All very well, Mr. Winthrop, and all very sorry. But my duty is quite clear. If she were an American citizen, there might be some question; she is a Mexican National. As to purchasing her freedom, the Secretary of War, I may inform you, has allotted to this survey the sum of forty thousand dollars. That must cover every expenditure, and only a fraction can go to trading goods. You saw for yourself that our presents were not enough to please the chief; we have still fifteen hundred miles to go, through one insatiable tribe after another."

How many human feelings have beaten, bruised, against the bars of military necessity! Caleb, with all the moral strength he had ever learned, tried again, but Captain Demerrit was short and final.

"Impossible. I have no authorization to purchase Indians' captives. This is the chief's woman, Mr. Winthrop, and to attempt to buy her would rouse him to dangerous hostility."

Night covers many things; the stars are very far and faint, and sometimes they are clouded. On the Llano, as under the elms, it may hide the sweetest things and the bitterest. It brings us all its nightmares and its inviting visions. If all is well, it brings us sleep, but to the tortured it can bring a kind of madness. Nor is there any torture like that of untried youth

brilliant circle of Kiowas, they were altered, their animal grace become brute strength, their eyes now cruel and cunning, and on the chief's breast the nobly-founded mission, as the woman was, of some butchered household.

And this she now told him. As my Pacific Report tells me, on Page 31: "She said that her name was Jose Maria; that she was from Rio de Naces; had been captured by the Kiowas when she was twenty and had lived with them seven years. Her beautiful boy is the son of the chief, but she wishes to leave her hard masters and accompany us, in the hope of again

Occasional setbacks slowed, but never stopped, the progress of America in general, or the railroads in particular.

when he has lost his way by the stars, when all that seemed fairest is suddenly revealed at its most hideous, when the strange woman troubles the blood and honor demands the impossible.

So, before the light, the sleepless Caleb like a sleepwalker threw back his blankets and stood up. Across the tent he saw that Doctor Marceau lay still. Out on the Llano a burrowing owl gave his high mellow quaver, and through the open tent flap a pale sunrise filled the east. It showed Caleb the dark familiar silhouette of Marceau's Army pistol in its holster hanging from the tent pole. The boy had never before picked up a weapon with intent to use it if he must, but the deathy touch of the cold metal went through his hot veins, steeling him in his purpose. He had no plan to kill, only to bargain at gun's point; a thunder like escaping hoofbeats pounded in his temples, as though the woman were already mounted behind him.

"Boy," came the quiet voice of the surgeon out of the gloom, "that weapon isn't loaded. And anyway, the hand of a man who hasn't slept all night isn't steady enough to shoot."

Old Doctor Winthrop, they say, when he entertained his classes with splendid tales of Western exploration, used to always tell that story. . . .

Those rails, I think, as I watch them dwindling behind us, have brought much more than they took away. They took away the stretches of blue gilia, and brought us wheat, which is also a flower, and gives us this day our daily bread. They took the Kiowas in all their painted splendor, and ended, too, their raids and the slavery and shame that woman knew. If she was left helpless behind, as the railroad survey went driving through, that is because civilization—a slow and halting progress, really—leaves many victims by the wayside, bits of the day's task that could not be accomplished because it was not God's will. For each of us, the doctor, the engineer, the scientist, can accomplish daily but one day's task, one *jornada*. Yet where that survey party crawled, our great trains fly now, crying their long clarion greeting to the future, and when across the land you hear it, that's America on its way. (1949)

Thirty Years with the Indian Tribes

Personal Memoirs of Henry R. Schoolcraft

Schoolcraft's account of life with the Ojibwa, "brief notices of passing events, facts and opinions," (1812—1842) inspired Longfellow's "The Song of Hiawatha."

1822. *July 9th.* The day which has closed has been a busy day, having been signalized as the date of my first public council with the Indians. It has ushered in my first diplomatic effort. For this purpose, all the bands present were invited to repair to camp, where Colonel Brady, at the appointed hour, ordered his men under arms, in full dress. They were formed in a hollow square in front of his marque. The American flag waved from a lofty staff. The day was bright and fine, and everything was well arranged to have the best effect upon the minds of the Indians. As the throng of both resident and foreign bands approached, headed by their chiefs, they were seated in the square. It was noticed that the chiefs were generally tall and striking-looking persons, of dignified manners, and well and even richly dressed. One of the chiefs of the home band, called Sassaba, appeared in a scarlet uniform, with epaulets and a sword. The other chiefs observed their native costume, which is, with this tribe, a toga of blue broad-cloth, folded and held by one hand on the breast, over a light-figured calico shirt, red cloth leggins and beaded moccasins, a belt or baldric about the waist, sustaining a knife-sheath and pouch, and a frontlet of skin or something of the sort, around the forehead, environed generally with eagles' feathers.

When the whole were seated, the colonel informed them that I had been sent by the great father, their President, to reside among them, that their respect was due me in that capacity, and that I would now address them. I had directed a quantity of tobacco to be laid before them; and offered them the pipe with the customary ceremonies. Being a novice in addresses of this kind, I had sat down early in the morning, in my crowded log hut, and written an address, couched in such a manner, and with such allusions and appeals, as I supposed would be most appropriate. I

was not mistaken, if I could judge by the responses made at the close of each sentence, as it was interpreted. The whole address was evidently well received, and responded to in a friendly manner, by the ruling chief, a tall, majestic, and graceful person named Shingabawossin, or the Image Stone.

Colonel Brady then made some remarks to the chiefs, dictated by the position he occupied as being about to take post, permanently, in their country. He referred to the treaty of purchase made at these falls two years before by Governor Cass. He told the Indians that he should not occupy their ancient encamping

W.H.D. Koerner (1878-1938)

Getting acquainted—it meant, for many a frontiers-man, re-forming his opinion of the "typical" Indian.

and burial-ground on the hill, but would select the next best site for his troops. This announcement was received with great satisfaction, as denoted by a heavy response of approbation on the part of the Indians; and the council closed to the apparent mutual satisfaction of all.

1822. *July 17th.* It is customary with the Chippewas at this place, when an inmate of the lodge is sick, to procure a thin sapling some twenty to thirty feet long, from which, after it has been trimmed, the bark is peeled. Native paints are then smeared over it as caprice dictates. To the slender top are then tied bits of scarlet, blue cloth, beads, or some other objects which are deemed acceptable to the manito or spirit, who has, it is believed, sent sickness to the lodge as a mark of his displeasure. The pole is then raised in front of the lodge and firmly adjusted in the ground. The sight of these manito poles gives quite a peculiar air to an Indian encampment.

Not knowing, however, the value attached to them, one of the officers, a few days after our arrival, having occasion for tent poles, sent one of his men for one of these poles of sacrifice; but its loss was soon observed by the Indians, who promptly reclaimed it, and restored it to the exact position which it occupied before.

There is, in fact, such a subtle and universal belief in the doctrine and agency of minor spirits of malign or benignant influence among the Indians who surround the cantonment, or visit the agency, and who are encamped at this season in great numbers in the open spaces of the village or its vicinity, that we are in constant danger of trespassing against some Indian cus-

tom, and of giving offence where it was least intended. It is said that one cause of the preference which the Indians have ever manifested for the French, is the respect which they are accustomed to pay to all their religious or superstitious observances, whereas an Englishman or an American is apt, either to take no pains to conceal his disgust for their superstitions, or to speak out bluntly against them.

1824. *May 30th.* Having found, in the circle of the Chippewa wigwams, a species of oral fictitious lore, I sent some specimens of it to friends in the lower country, where the subject excited interest. "I am anxious," writes a distinguished person, under this date, "that you should bring with you, when you come down, your collection of Indian tales. I should be happy to see them."

That the Indians should possess this mental trait of indulging in lodge stories, impressed me as a novel characteristic, which nothing I had ever heard of the race had prepared me for. I had always heard the Indian spoken of as a revengeful, bloodthirsty man, who was steeled to endurance and delighted in deeds of cruelty. To find him a man capable of feelings and affections, with a heart open to the wants, and responsive to the ties of social life, was amazing. But the surprise reached its acme, when I found him whiling away a part of the tedium of his long winter evenings in relating tales and legends for the amusement of the lodge circle. These fictions were sometimes employed, I observed, to convey instruction, or impress examples of courage, daring, or right action. But they were, at all times, replete with the wild forest notions of the spiritual agencies, necromancy, and, demonology. abundantly the hopes and notions of a and his belief future

They revealed causes of his fears—his Deity, in a state.

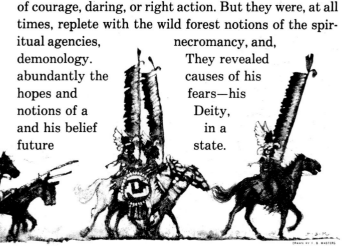

Grounds of Fear

A Letter from a Chippewa Chieftain

The "hunger and thirst of the white man for the Indian's land is almost equal to his hunger and thirst after righteousness." (Grover Cleveland, 1887). Today the Chippewa (or "Ojibwa") number 30,000 in the U.S. and are scattered on reservations throughout five states.

I will give you the grounds of my fears why the Indians will never have a permanent hold upon any part of the Western country, unless by special act of the U.S. Congress.

For years, the fires of the Indian lodge have been removed west. Their rights have been trampled upon by settlers, and this, with other annoyances, has ever unsettled the minds of the Indians. The consequence has been and ever will be that they will remove, step by step, to escape this annoyance.

The present belief of the Western and Southwestern nations is that they will never again be moved, and that the land they now occupy will be theirs forever. What sort of guarantee do they have of their continuing on their land unmolested? Will not the same plea that was given to remove the Massachusetts, New York, Ohio and Georgia Indians—will not the same plea of necessity (and, as some say, an act of kindness to them) be urged on those on the other side of The Father of Waters as has been urged on this side? If not

this—enterprise, yes, Yankee enterprise, will require railroads to be laid out, canals to be opened, military roads cut through the land of the Indians in the West, and their land must either be bought from them or taken. And when this is done, or commenced to be done, they will cease to work in their lands, since such labor would not be in their benefit, but for those who must occupy it when they leave it. The delightful fields of the Indians in Georgia were the greatest objects which the white men desired for themselves.

There is a rich spot of land this side of the desert below the Rocky Mountains, the only rich land, and the Indian has been placed on this like a barrier. The land so occupied, *if not cultivated*, the paleface will reason himself into the idea that the Great Spirit intended to make the whole of North America a farmland and thereby justify himself for taking to till what the Indian could not improve.

Necessity will oblige the Indian to sell. Our Fathers sold their lands to the government and lived on the proceeds of this sale, and soon the government will want to buy *this land*, and our children will live on the annuities as we do now on ours. So, they will fare no worse than we have. In this way, they will become impoverished, and will have to sell their lands piece by piece, until all is gone and they suffer. (1850)

Hard Winter

A Tale told by Oliver La Farge

He saw his wife start backing her horse out of the packed circle of mounted Indians and wagons, and without ceasing to sing, he turned his head slightly to watch her. The horse, nervous from the crowd, answered uncertainly, with shifting forefeet and resistant tossings of the head which made the bells on his bridle ring together. She forced the animal back with a firm hand, turning in the saddle to speak laughingly to those behind her; then getting clear of the narrowest press, she wheeled sharply, heading toward her tepee.

The song ended. Tall Walker looked around to watch her pass along the skyline, a satisfaction in him at the sight of her, the very type of a young Jicarilla Apache wife. She sat her horse firmly, easily, riding with high bridle hand and slack rein. Her heavy, black hair hung in two braids, intertwined with ribbon; above the meeting of the braids was a red celluloid comb. A circular design was painted on each cheek, and three red lines drawn on her chin. Across her shoulders she wore the yoke of gold-colored buckskin with wide, curving bands of beadwork and the long fringe hanging down each arm to her wrists. About her waist, covering her saddle and skirts, were draped gay blankets of strong design, beneath which her feet showed in gayly beaded moccasins. Her horse moved easily at the jog trot, with tinkling bells. She was going to prepare food. Tall Walker, considering himself, found that he was moderately hungry and would soon be more so.

The drums began again, he returned to singing. His uncle, an elderly man, and another slightly younger one were drumming; Tall Walker and about six others made up the chorus as many more danced, according to their mood —all

Llaneros, plainsmen, celebrating their victory in the sacred race that morning.

A young man danced gracefully, stripped to the waist. He wore a horsehair roach and a feather on his head, blue work pants, moccasins. Another sported a brilliant flannel shirt; another a buckskin jacket, cloth leggings and big hat.

They danced all together or by turns, without fixed order. Laughter came readily. Around the performers were ranked mounted Indians, Indians afoot and in wagons, and a few intrusive, alien-seeming motors. The people crowded together, the Apache tribe and their guests—Navajos, Tewas, Keres, Taos, a couple of Utes, Mexicans, and a few Anglo-Americans. The spectators formed a mass with jingling bridles, fretting hoofs, men, women, children, dark faces, big hats, bright blankets, a constant upraising of dust clouds in the noon sunshine. It was the Apache fiesta.

A slender young man with a white blanket wrapped about himself and over his head sat down beside Tall Walker. The Apache turned and saw a handsome, aquiline face, cut off at the line of the ear lobe by a neatly wrapped braid. There was yellow paint on the forehead, yellow and red on each cheek. He stopped singing and extended his hand. Their hands touched, clasped lightly, and remained so while they smiled.

"Como' stamos?" the man asked.

"Bueno. Y tu?"

"Bueno."

They used the simplified Spanish which is the intertribal language of New Mexico.

"When I didn't see you this morning, I thought you would not come at all. What kept you?"

"Mud by Horse Lake; it held us up. We came in a motor. Are there many others here from Taos?"

"Three or four, I think. Will you sing?"

"All right."

While they talked, Tall Walker had noticed changes about his friend; a fat look, though he was not fat; something curious in his expression. The man wore blue-flannel leggings with beadwork strips, and fine moccasins, unusually showy for one who was traveling, even a Taos Indian.

Tall Walker reached over and touched the old drummer's elbow.

"My uncle, here is Juan from Taos. He will sing."

Moccasins thump, raising the ground to dust; glistening beads dance on motley costumes; different tongues sing songs in unison. A feast of sights and sounds.
An Apache fiesta.

The old man turned, smiling, "Good. Do you know the song?"

Juan nodded consent. "Surely."

The singers shifted their places slightly to make room for the visitor. The drums intoned a few beats, establishing the feel of the rhythm. Juan sang the introduction alone, a phrase of music carried on pure vowel sounds; the clear voice of a first-rate Taos singer rang out sweetly, holding attention, inspiring the dancers' feet to move. At the end of the phrase, the chorus took up the song, livelier under his leadership. Tall Walker, singing, remembered Indian-school days, and thought how far they had traveled from the two unhappy children who made friends there.

At the next pause, he said, "My tepee is right over there. Come eat with us in a little while."

Juan answered, "I shall visit you, but I am camped on that side. A white woman is with us; I eat with her."

His hesitation over the last sentence caught the Apache's attention, causing him to want to ask a question, then decide not to.

"This is our fiesta," he said; "we have plenty. Let her come too."

"Perhaps. She might like it. She wants to know about Indians, all kinds of Indians."

The insistent drums broke in upon them, and their talk ceased.

The sun had moved to the middle of the western sky; the crowd had thinned and some of the dancers dropped out when Tall Walker stood up.

"I am hungry, and I know where food is. Are you coming?"

"All right."

They went together to the Apache's tepee, standing on the ridge overlooking all the eastern part of the encampment and the quiet, blue-shining lake about the muddy shores of which many horses drifted. The baby slept in its cradle board; his young daughter staggered about holding onto a puppy's tail; his wife lifted a pot off the fire and set goat's ribs to broil. Although she, too, had been to school, she greeted Juan modestly in Spanish and went on cooking. The two men reclined in the shade of the tepee's entrance.

Juan said, "It seems to be a good fiesta."

Tall Walker paused a moment before replying. He heard the drums and singing softly, like a central *motif* about which cohered the sounds of the encampment—a horse neighing, voices, laughter, a child crying, dogs, the tinkle of sleigh bells on bridles, and jerky clangor of cowbells on grazing horses. He saw the tents and tall, white tepees, wagons, the smoke of hundreds of fires, the patched-together shelters of brush and cloth that the Navajos put up, the medicine-men's inclosure of green branches, dotted without form or arrangement on the gray-green slopes and ridges about the north end of the lake, and yet achieving complete satisfaction of form to the eye. In and out of the camps wove a pattern of moving people, afoot or mounted, singly or in groups, bright blankets, brilliant dresses of women, the varying splendors of men of different tribes. The smell of food smote his nostrils sweetly.

"It is a good fiesta; everybody is happy and many people have come. But we don't get any whisky this year; the new agent, he has men watching all around."

"Yes, some men searched our car when we came in."

Tall Walker's wife served food. Juan threw back the fine, white blanket he had worn wrapped about himself, Taos fashion, and during the silence of serious eating the Apache could take the full measure of his friend's prosperity. Juan wore a shirt of green silk, cut in the Indian manner, a silk scarf at his throat, a coral necklace and several rings. At his waist he had a belt studded with brass and vari-colored glass knobs, on it two cartridge clips and an automatic with mother-of-pearl handle. His countenance agreed with the dress; though he was not fat, and his profile was aquiline, his face had filled out; under the painted decoration his skin was sleek.

His host was in striking contrast. For finery he had only a beaded waistcoat, worn over a red-and-black-checked flannel shirt, and a couple of feathers stuck in his floppy old black felt hat. His blue work trousers were worn and faded, his feet incased in old, brown shoes. Characteristically, the Taos Indian's hair was neat and shiny, the braids in perfect order, while the Apache's had a shaggy look. Tall Walker's face showed the tribal expression of hunger and capacity for war. His wife was dressed well, perhaps even expensively so, but Juan wore solid money, the value of sheep and horses, upon his person.

They consumed meat, chili, melons and black coffee; then relaxed digestively over cigarettes.

Tall Walker said, "You are rich."

"I shall be, perhaps. She gives me these things, that white woman."

"Who is she? Why does she do it?"

"Oh, I'm just working for her. Guiding—that is, I take her places like here, and drive her car, and explain things to her. It's a good job, and besides these things, I have earned a gun and a saddle."

He spoke like a man withholding something.

Tall Walker said, "You know how to drive a car?"

"Yes, I learned that last year."

"I should like to know that."

Juan changed the subject. They exchanged news of other friends, particularly those with whom they had gone through the misery of school, referring to them, as they did to each other, by their Spanish names. Juan called Tall Walker "Celestino." They spoke of the sheep and crops and the hunting season. At length Juan rose, gathering his blanket round him.

"I must go back to our camp now. Come along. There may be something good to eat, and there will be people."

"Good." The Apache rose. "Let us go over."

The car, with an olive-green tent attached to it, was parked in a place well chosen to give a view while yet standing withdrawn from the smells, noises and dogs of the encampment. Around an almost dead fire were sprawled three Taos Indians, an elderly Navajo, and a white woman, eating grapes which they had purchased from a Zia peddler, who sat with them, his unsold fruit in a box behind him.

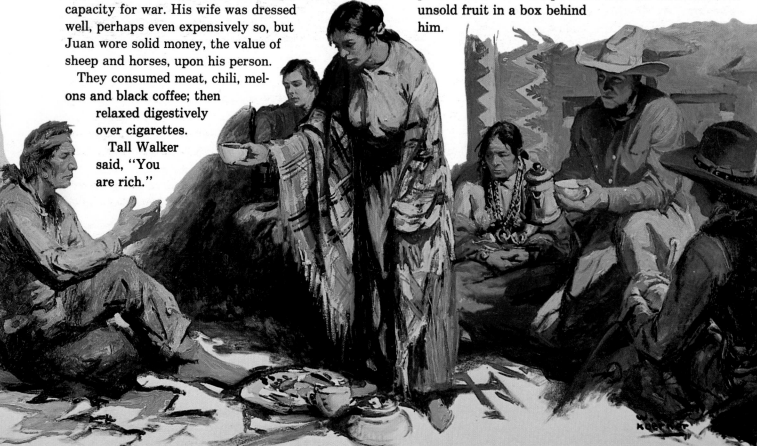

W.H.D. Koerner (1878-1938)

Tall Walker knew everyone there at least slightly, save the woman. Her he studied in the intervals of a desultory conversation in which he took little part, since it was conducted in English—a language he used but seldom nowadays. He was struck first by the fact that she was wearing moccasins and the red-and-blue blanket which the Kiowas and some Taos affect. This was incongruous. She was older than he or Juan, and yet immature. Clearly there had been no childbearing to spread her figure or mark her face, no hard work, nothing to age her. She was girlish, and at the same time she was older than broad-hipped, drudging Apache mothers of the same years. Plainly, she thought that Indians were very important, and was enjoying herself playing Indian. She had welcomed him, Celestino, in a fluttery, excited manner, with some joking remark about Apaches spoken too quickly for him to understand. He was amused and curious.

A young man joined them from a neighboring motor camp. He was blonde, tall, and dressed ostentatiously in part Indian costume, like the woman. Those Indians he knew he hailed by name, making a great point of shared jokes and common interests, displaying an eager familiarity which they met politely.

He had seen such white people fussing around Taos when he visited there; they seemed to be a special tribe. The Taos people treated them with forbearance, keeping them outside of everything important and bearing with their stupidities.

Navajos and Apaches understand each other's languages. The elderly Navajo said to him, "What is this *Bellicana* in the Taos clothes? Is he a half man?"

"Just a little crazy, I think," Tall Walker answered. "They say there are many of them around Taos. That woman too. They are very fond of Indians, it seems."

The Navajo spat. "Very fond. That woman is so fond she's likely to have a baby, I think."

Tall Walker smiled. It was true. Juan was not just working for her. She was in love with him, and she was satisfied. So the women give you presents to do that.

She was in love with Juan, but what about him? He liked her well enough, one could see, but it was not love, nor yet the attitude of any man settled in marriage. There was a hidden shame present, a watchfulness of people. Juan had glanced around quickly when they laughed, but she understood neither Navajo nor Apache. Tall Walker spat out a grape skin. Those other Taos, they had mockery hidden under their blankets for the white man and woman; but for the man of their own tribe. . .one could not be sure; they would not display themselves before strangers.

The woman spoke to him. "Are you coming to the Taos fiesta next month, Celestino?"

"I don't know. I got to take care of my sheep."

Juan said in English, "You better come. We got a

W.H.D. Koerner (1878-1938)

The part Indian costume accentuated her whiteness.

big house, you know, and plenty hay for your horse. You come and stay with us. We can have a drink."

He greatly desired to see more of these strange people. "All right. I'll come that time. I see you there." He rose. "I got to go to my house now."

To the Navajo, he said, "I am camped over yonder; come if you want. There is food. I shall be there until the dancing starts again."

The man grunted. "Good, I shall come, perhaps. I may want somewhere to lie down and laugh."

The sun was down; fires began to count as golden spots in the blue dusk; where there were fires inside the tepees, the great cones glowed softly at the base, their peaks shadowy. At his camp, his wife was rocking the baby, his daughter slept on a sheepskin. As he sat down beside her, he thought, "Juan has nothing."

The round dance lasted from an hour after dark until midnight. About halfway between then and dawn the last stubborn celebrants gave over their singing and left the bonfires to die away. The fiesta was ended.

People arose lazily, relaxed by enjoyment, and short

of sleep. The tepees began to be struck a few hours after sunrise, and piecemeal the encampment dissolved into two streams of wagons and mounted men along the dusty road north and south from the lake. Tall Walker turned his wagon aside at a dim cart track up which they drove, arriving at their small log cabin in the mid-afternoon. Finery was laid aside; they reentered normal life. Long days without event with the sheep on the thinly wooded mountain slopes; evenings of well-fed fatigue, a little talk, a little playing with the children; nights of deep sleep; and always, first and central, the sheep. Later the sale of the lamb crop would bring them in to the post trader at Dulce, and later still there would be camp life again, when they moved to the winter range.

Two days beforehand, Tall Walker announced that he was going to the Taos fiesta. His wife said she would not go; there was no relative near who could be trusted with the sheep, and besides, the baby was so young, it ought not to be always traveling. He agreed, although he had been inclined to argue that in olden days women and babies traveled all the time. But she was right about the sheep, and to him, too, the welfare of his little son was of the first importance. He had been disappointed when his first child was a girl, and he wanted the boy to grow well. Besides, his wife was a person who knew her own mind and had plenty of sense. Now that girls went to school, it was different from the old times when they just took orders; though a man would not admit that before other men.

He made the ride to Taos in a day and a half, starting one afternoon and arriving the next day just before sunset. Had a white man covered the ground in the same time, it would have been a record; had he arrived feeling as fresh as the Apache did, he would have become famous for his endurance.

Even from a distance, as he rode between the two piled-up masses of Taos Pueblo, one could tell that he was not a native of the place. Slouching comfortably in the saddle, his wide shoulders and heavy-boned frame dwarfed his pony. The big, shapeless hat proclaimed his tribe from afar; near to, one noticed his dark, broad face, and felt forcefulness, that effect of fitness for war which was not an individual characteristic but an emanation from the personality of his tribe. For this visit he had wrapped his   braids with otter

fur trimmed with beads, and borrowed a showy pair of moccasins. Added to his handsome waistcoat, the effect was good, although his trousers still plainly indicated a poor man. Most Apaches are poor.

He kept his eye out for acquaintances, having an unexpected feeling that he did not want to ask a stranger the way to that woman's house. Shortly he encountered a man he knew well, who had played football beside him for two seasons on the Santa Fe team. He reined in his horse and raised a hand.

"*Como' stamos?*" It passed through his mind that he ought to practice speaking English, but he was reluctant to do so. Spanish came easily.

"*Bueno. Y tu?*"

"*Bueno.*"

They shook hands and chatted. The Taos, whose Spanish name was Fulgencio Mirabal, invited him to stay at his house.

"I promised Juan I would stay with him."

"Which Juan?"

"Juan Sota. Where does he live now?"

"Oh, that one," Fulgencio paused. "Go right on, then take a road to the right by two cottonwoods, and pretty soon you see a Mexican house with an arched gateway, so"—and moved his hands descriptively.

Tall Walker said "*Bueno.* I want to see."

Ten years ago they had known each other as intimately as tribal differences and the harsh restrictions of the school would allow. They esteemed each other's opinion. Fulgencio said, pulling his blanket up over his shoulders:

"We feel badly about Juan, the people here." He paused. "Well, I'll see you tomorrow."

"*Bueno. Hasta luego.*"

Perhaps Fulgencio was right. But then, a man takes what he can get; and if the white woman is rich and a fool, why not? One would not want to go on like that, of course. He found the place, then tied his horse at the gate and entered the yard, which was pleasantly shaded by cottonwoods. He saw no one. The door was big, carved and painted. He liked that, although he thought the paint too faded. Behind this door was a strange life; something to see, examine, perhaps enjoy, perhaps laugh at, and to tell about afterward. Life is monotonous,   novelty a pleasure. He knocked.

A Mexican woman

Hard lines in his countenance emanated a characteristic forcefulness derived from generations of hard living.

Beyond the peaceful setting of the Mexican village dwelt a tribe of white people with its own incongruous customs.

let him in and left him standing, hat in hand, in the hall. The stolid, rather stupid expression of his face disguised embarrassment, a certain awkwardness arising from the elegance of the place. He heard voices speaking English in the high, clear tones which are so unlike Indian conversation, then laughter, followed by a pause as the maid entered the room and someone's exclamation, "An Apache!" Juan came into the hall, saying cordially, *"Llega, 'migo."*

Following his friend, he stepped over the threshold of a doorway the frame of which he filled for a moment as he paused, looking about him before he entered a place, and a period, of so much novelty and so many impressions that not until long after did he sort them out. Right at the outset he encountered numbers of people gathered together, women similar to Juan's, too rapid talk, a drink of whisky with which began a long-continuing sense of unreality.

It was a tribe of white people, with its own strange manners and incomprehensible customs. Some of them had a remarkable knowledge of and sympathy for Indians. Others were abysmally ignorant. Some worked—many at painting—some seemed to have no occupation at all. In two things, they were all alike—that much of their conversation seemed to be made for its own sake, without need, and that they all set tremendous store by Indians.

The Taos people were tolerant of them; indebted to some for real services to their Pueblo, fond of some, forbearing with others. But Tall Walker had little time for talking with the Taos, save when they came to visit. The fiesta passed as a mere background to his new explorations; he stayed on one day and another, a third and a fourth. A painter gave him money to pose. People wanted to hear him sing, to ask about the customs of his tribe. They tickled his vanity, and from time to time gave him drinks. He observed, he laughed within himself, he enjoyed, and he was confused.

Many people stayed late at one woman's house, and he, Juan, and Juan's woman stayed till the last. These two women were so similar in expression that at first he had taken them for sisters, although their features were quite unlike. He had heard that his hostess had had an affair with a Taos man once, but his family had talked him out of it. She had been making up to Tall Walker for the last few days.

As they, the last of the visitors, got ready to go, he was tipsy. When she came up to him, he saw her through a warm glow, and it occurred to him that a white woman might be desirable.

She said, "Why don't you stay here?"

He stood facing her for some time before he answered, while through his mind ran summations of what he had been vaguely thinking these last days: "I'm not going to be like Juan....One time, why not?...I'm a man....It doesn't matter...."

He said, "All right."

She called loudly to the others, "Celestino isn't going with you."

That shamelessness caused him a wave of embarrassed anger, and he did not hear what was answered.

He thought, "If I go now, it will look as if I were afraid to sleep with a woman." The outer door shut, and she handed him another drink, saying, "Sit down."

He took the drink, but remained stolid with annoyance. Perplexed, she made conversation which fell flat. She suggested that he sing some more, pointing to the fine drum she had—an instrument which he had been enjoying. He refused with a brusque "No." Then she was angry and turned sharp, scolding. He rose to his feet, silent, dangerous, and stepped toward her. Re-

strictions which had guarded her all her life were non-existent to this half-intoxicated Apache. She drew in her breath sharply and became meek. Even confused as he was, he could feel that he had taken her prisoner.

He stayed on at that house. She gave him Indian finery, and a rifle, and she surrounded him with unimagined luxury. Within a few days his eyes were opened to a scale of spending money which, even when he saw it, he could hardly believe. "I shall stay a few days," he thought; "I shall gather goods and money."

Dressed in Indian perfection to the last detail, save for the huge hat, with which he refused to part, she took him, a slightly bewildered clothes horse, to Santa Fe. He enjoyed the motor ride, and seeing that city again, and the novelty of the huge hotel, in which he twice got lost. He found that people's attitude toward him was equivocal, but he drew plenty of attention, which pleased him, and the rest he ignored. After about a week, they returned to Taos. He thought it was about time to go home, but two more artists wanted to paint him. That was easy money, and flattering. He was beginning to feel very important. It was a pleasant, easy, luxurious life; the woman was much in love with him, it seemed. In early November he was still there, and the woman was talking of taking him to New York. He would like to see that place.

He went over to visit Juan one day, to plan a hunting trip, and the Taos handed him a letter, saying, "This came for you." It was addressed to "Celestino Roman, c/o Juan Sota, Taos P.O., New Mexico." He had never received a letter before, it made him uneasy. The stamp was red and had Washington on it. He wondered if that meant it came from the Indian Office. A sense of guilt stole over him. Back at the house he opened it and read it slowly, with difficulty:

JICARILLA, DULCE P.O.
NEW MEXICO
November 8

Dear Friend Husband: I take my pen to say I am well an hope You are the Same. Agent say we got to move ship to Winter Range rigt now or he men will move them ship for us those Men is rough if they move our ship we might lose some. I think goöou come back now an move ship you been gone long time I not know where are you Please come back rigt now. Little girl is well baby sick a little I come into Doctor he give me some Medcin an I write this. Come back and move ship. I send this to Juan get you. Trader write it address for me. I will close now wit best regards

yours loving wife
ANTONIA MARIANO

A letter is a strange thing; it has power. This one found its way to Taos and to Juan, told Juan to give it

The sheep—not a livelihood, but a way of life for the Apaches, the base for their economy, their means of survival.

to him, and he opened it and his wife spoke to him. So the baby, the boy, was sick a little, but the doctor had given him medicine. The doctor was good; the baby would be all right. He went into the living room where the white woman was.

"I got a letter. I got to move my sheep onto the winter range."

"A letter? From whom?" Her voice was sharp.

"My wife, she write it."

The woman lit a cigarette and spoke again calmly, with a soft voice, which he liked: "You are going back to your wife?"

"I got to move my sheep and my horses. If they stay on that summer range, maybe it snow hard, maybe then they can't eat. I might lose them. If I don't move them, those government men, they will do it. They're rough. I go tomorrow."

"How many sheep have you?"

"I got three hundred, and I got twenty horses."

"That's not many."

"When I start in, when they divide up the sheep that time, I got fifty head. Now I got three hundred. Pretty soon I have maybe a thousand, have cattle, plenty horses, like Agapito and them fellers. It's what we eat sometimes, the sheep, and we sell wool and the lambs, and that way we got money to buy flour and what we need, all us Apaches. Before we didn't have no sheep, sometimes we were starving; we didn't have no money at all. Just some old clothes and a little food Washington gave us, that's all. A lot of people died then. I guess about half the Apaches died. Maybe we don't take good care of our sheep, we got to eat grass ourselves then, I guess."

He explained thus carefully, knowing how deeply ignorant she was. He wanted her to know and to feel as she should. The woman listened with nervous patience.

She said, "But you don't have to count on the sheep now. Why, I could buy your whole flock. You are through with all that work and trouble now. You can have anything you want. If you want to send money to your wife, I can give it to you. Let the sheep go."

He regarded her blankly. What she suggested was unnatural, incomprehensible.

She rose. "Don't you like it here?"

He liked it very much; it was better than anything he had ever known or dreamed of. "Yeh, it's all right."

She spoke softly, "And I? Do you not care for me?"

Her behavior was queer, but she could not help that. He was very fond of her; she was the symbol of comfort and there was no little passion shared.

"Yeh, I like you all right."

She sighed. "Why are you going?"

He felt sorry for her. She didn't understand, and was unhappy about it. He did not want to cause her pain.

"I got to move those sheep and those horses. We go down on south half of the reservation, we get settled there. Then pretty soon I guess I come back here. I just want to move my sheep, that's all."

"Then you'll come back?"

"Yeh, I come back all right."

"All right, but don't fail. And it doesn't matter how many sheep you lose; I'll make it up to you."

His horse was in fine shape, almost too fat. Although the days were short, their coolness even at noon made traveling easy, and yet he minded the journey much more than formerly, finding that long hours in the saddle irked him, and he grew tired easily. He wore

good, heavy American clothes, suitable for winter work, his new rifle was under his leg, and there were dollars in his pocket. The rest of his finery he had left behind. On the second morning, the sky was clear and hard, with streaks of wind cloud in the northwest. "It's going to be a hard winter," he thought.

He arrived home at noon. His wife received him quietly, remarking, "You were away a long time." He showed her his money, rifle and new clothes, told of sitting for the painters and said it had been worthwhile. He was uneasy, conscious of unasked questions, unspoken thoughts.

The little girl was well and lively, but the baby was fretful. It worried and disturbed him to see his son in poor health; he had convinced himself that the child would be well by the time he got back. During the night it cried a good deal. He was restless on the hard floor; supper had seemed coarse and unappetizing; the cabin was bleak, too small, dirty; his wife was stolid, shabby, and did not give the adulation to which he was accustomed. He had found a better life elsewhere, to which he would soon return.

He overslept, waking finally to the sound of her movements about the rickety stove. They started early, she driving the wagon, he on horseback, herding the horses and sheep. It gave him plenty to do.

By mid-morning the sky was gray and lowering, with a bitter, cold wind under it. About noon the wind slackened and it began to snow; dry, heavy flakes pouring down thickly. When they made camp, the ground was already covered a couple of inches deep, the sheep had not eaten well during the day, and it was still snowing. They had both of them felt the pinch of the cold, she especially so when she sat driving. The baby was cross and fed poorly. They talked about the weather, hoping this would not last. His appetite was restored to him, and he found the simple food delicious.

When he went out at sunrise, the snow was nearly a foot deep where it had not drifted, and still coming down, but less rapidly. One old ewe had died. The horses he found without difficulty, bunched under the lee of a steepish hill. They had fared moderately well. They turned into a long, wide valley leading southward, following the faint

depression in the snow which showed that others had been along the road the day before. The sky cleared, the white flakes ceased falling, the sun took effect. By noon the top of the snow was beginning to melt. Save for worrying about their son, who still did not feed well, they felt quite cheerful.

"When we get down there and stop traveling," he said, "he'll get well."

Then the wind sprang up again, driving, and with it a cold which was not a knife but a bludgeon beating upon them. They wrapped the children in everything they could, though they themselves were none too warm. With the wind came more snow, thick and blinding. One could hardly believe how fast it came. In the valley it drifted deep on top of other drifts, but even if they could have made their way along the rough ground on the ridges, they could not have faced the wind there. The string of horses became hard to manage, the sheep huddled in a dense mass, moving by inches. If the flock was to be saved, it was vital to get them over the few score miles to where the south half dipped to lower, warmer elevations and the tall grass could be reached all winter.

He drove his loose horses mercilessly into the deepening drifts to make a road. When he had it trampled down, he would go back to help his wife. She alternated between driving the wagon and herding the reluctant sheep along. When she sat on the wagon box his heart was wrung for her, since in those minutes without activity the cold went right through her. In his own discomfort, he thought bitterly of what he had abandoned to submit himself to this, and would double his efforts to get it over and to return to luxury.

They were exhausted by the time they reached a thick bunch of trees, in the shelter where they pitched camp. He built huge bonfires to warm the sheep and worked long trying to clear ground so that they could graze. Near sunset another family, Roan Horse and his wife, joined them. Roan Horse had two strong sons, but they were away at school. The two groups pitched in together, gathering fuel and clearing ground. The newcomer had some hay in his wagon, which they fed to their teams and best saddle horses. Tall Walker had lost a score or more of sheep during the afternoon.

His infant son cried through most of the night.

His wife said, "I think my milk is no good now. I was so cold sometimes." He spoke comfortingly and urged her to eat. Then, exhausted, he fell asleep, dimly aware that she watched late and tended the fire.

In the morning there were more sheep and one horse frozen. The wind had let up, but the snow continued, thick, soft and unmerciful. They could not stay where they were; their animals would starve and be snowed in. This day's drive should get them to lower country. So the two families pushed on together.

They had never seen such snow. Always it was up to the horses' bellies, sometimes they floundered in drifts saddle-high, and in a few places it was as high as a mounted man. The hungry horses weakened, faltered and gave up; one by one they became exhausted, standing with lowered heads, already half frozen. Only the teams and the mounts they rode, which had been given hay, and to which now they fed bread and anything else they could find, kept going. The two men charged and charged at the drifts breaking trail. The sheep followed reluctantly, leaving behind a scattering trail of frozen corpses. Tall Walker's horse, with a month of oats and alfalfa behind it, stood up remarkably well. It disturbed him to see his wife's drawn, worried expression. No complaint passed her lips, but she was visibly weary as she struggled with the flocks, and miserable with cold when she drove, urging on the team with her arm worn out from whipping. He did not like to ask after the boy.

They camped again, with huge fires for the remnant of their flocks—but little over half of the original number. For warmth, they set up but one tepee, in which they maintained a good blaze. They brought into cover with them a couple of good ewes which were particularly weak. Roan Horse's wife helped with the baby. Tall Walker was accustomed to seeing it pink, plump and vociferous. Now its skin was tight over its face, and greenish in color; its eyes were too large; it whimpered steadily and feebly. Roan Horse's solid wife was visibly moved, and under the wisps of disordered hair which fell over her face, Tall Walker could see that his wife wept silently. The little girl seemed hungry and cross, but well enough.

He and Roan Horse prayed for the sheep, for themselves, for Tall Walker's son, for other Apaches caught in the storm. As they concentrated on their solemn chanting, the fire warmed their knees and faces, and the bitter cold pressed heavily against their backs.

There was scarcely a quarter of their flocks alive the next morning. Roan Horse's saddle pony was dead. The two men and the remaining saddle horse broke trail until the horse went down in the soft snow of a deep, hidden arroyo. They worked hard, but the animal would not help itself, and at length they abandoned it, already half asleep. They struggled on foot, leading the wagon teams over each piece of ground gained. Then the sheep stopped. Starved and half frozen, the animals simply stood still. They loaded a few of their best ewes onto the wagons, and Roan Horse took a young ram, and they went on to try to save themselves. By noon it had stopped snowing, but the cold continued. Digging and chopping where wind had swept the snow thin, they got up a few armfuls of grass for the teams.

A couple of hours after that, and about five miles from their last camp, they came on a trail already

Tall Walker risks the lives of his family to save their future; the lamb, like his baby son, requires special care.

made, with but little fresh snow on it. Here the wagons could make reasonable speed, with much beating of the horses, although dead sheep lay under the trampled trail so thickly as to make the footing really perilous.

They smelled wood smoke in the clear air. Then, with the sun halfway across the winter sky, they saw a group of a score or more tepees and tents ahead of them under the shelter of a bluff, a bunch of about fifty sheep huddled together, some horses and, most remarkable of all, two automobiles.

Tall Walker was walking beside the wagon team, whip in hand. Now he looked up at his wife anxiously.

"How is my boy?"

"He is breathing." She was crying again.

"Perhaps the doctor will be there. Those are Government cars."

They jolted on over hard snow and frozen sheep, over the dead livelihood of the Apache tribe. Most of the people at the camp were busy around the little band of animals or at the automobiles. Something was being handed out. The agent came on horseback to meet them; he was haggard and unshaven.

"I'm glad to see you," he said. "There are still many people not accounted for. Have you anything left?"

"We got three ewes in the wagon. They're all right."

"Are you people all right?"

Tall Walker looked at his wife. She had stopped crying and was staring hard at nothing. Slowly she turned her face toward him.

"My little boy, he's died."

"That's too bad. I'm sorry." In the last forty-eight hours, the agent had seen so much tragedy that he had lost his capacity for receiving it. The whole winter range was under six feet of snow; his Indians were destitute; many families were still to be found. He anaesthetized himself with relentless effort. "I'm sorry," he repeated. "We have feed for your stock here, put them with the bunch, and you can get food and some clothing from those cars. There is more coming. The doctor is at another camp, down below; he will be here this evening, if anyone is sick."

"All right. I think by and by he might look at my wife, maybe."

The agent glanced at her. "Yes. I'll tell him." He spurred his mount and rode over to talk to Roan Horse.

Tall Walker's wife sat without moving until he touched her arm, saying, "We must make camp."

He led the team off the road and started to unharness it.

"You put up the tepee," he said. "I'll get the animals fed, and see about this food for us."

She set to work without speaking. He paused to look at her, seeing the disheveled hair hanging all about her head, the pinched, drawn face, the self-control and the steadiness with which she went about her business. "That is how Apache women are," he thought; "that is why we were great warriors once."

He took the horses over and saw them fed. His wife had the lodge poles out, and, with the help of a couple of other women, was arranging the canvas.

More cars arrived, and he stopped to watch them—two big trucks, staggering, plunging and throwing up snow. Taking a ewe on his   shoulders, he started over.

Behind the trucks followed a big sedan which he recognized. He stopped again, midway of the camp.

The sedan turned out to pass the trucks, and then came slowly along past the cluster of tents. He could see the white woman staring out of the front window beside Juan, who was driving. It was Juan who recognized him. The car stopped and she got out. He thought, inconsequently, that he had not known she owned such sensible clothing. The face of the world had been altered, but her big car remained, the token of a house with many fireplaces, of comfort and an end to effort in Taos whence it came. Aeons had passed, but she was just the same as ever. There was the contradictory appearance of being worn out and of immaturity, and the eager, blue eyes.

She said, "Celestino! You poor dear, you look done in. I was so worried about you when I heard how terrible the storm was. I came as soon as I could. I have food and clothing for you, and you must come back to my house. Are you all right?"

"I guess I'm all right."

"Did you lose your sheep?"

"I lost them, and I lost my horses. Only just three ewes we brought in the wagon. All the Apaches, they lost their sheep; only this little bunch here, that's all."

"Thank heaven, you don't need to worry. I shall take care of you. Now come with me. You don't need sheep any longer."

He studied her gravely, with a blank face. From where he stood, he could see his wife carrying a bundle of blankets and a kettle into the tepee, and the little girl running after her. He shifted the ewe on his shoulders, feeling its weak heartbeats against his face. For a long time he had not felt any emotion; he had just known that things had happened, and that they were bad. Since back before the sheep stopped moving he had been numb. Now suddenly he was angry—so deeply, tremendously angry that he shook and he could not speak at all. As if in a mist, he saw her step back from him with startled face. He got control of himself by an effort and, turning away, walked off to take the ewe to be fed. The woman called after him, but he gave no sign of hearing her.

(1933)

They Came
for *Free Land*

Free Land

A Proclamation by the Post

With its customary generosity the United States Government will soon give away, absolutely free, fifteen thousand farms consisting of one hundred and sixty acres each.

In August of the present year the reservation purchased from the Kiowa, Comanche and Apache Indians at a cost of three million dollars will be thrown open to settlement by white citizens, and these farms will pass into possession of those who reach them first. The land is located in the southern part of Oklahoma Territory and is easily accessible by railroad and wagon route. Already thousands are making this new country their Mecca, and the long string of covered wagons wending across the prairies of Kansas and Oklahoma, en route, reminds one very much of the days when the Cherokee Strip was opened. The Cherokee Strip, or Outlet, was opened in 1893, and six million acres of tillable land was given to white people. Fifty thousand men, women and children took part in that famous race, and from the manner in which they are now rushing toward the Kiowa and Comanche reservation borders, fully that number will race again. As there are only fifteen thousand farms, and fully that number of people are already along the borders, there will not be enough land to go around.

The result will be that more land must be taken from the Indians, and it will not be long before there is not a remaining Indian reservation in the West.

Three thousand civilized Indians of the Kiowa, Comanche and Apache tribes have been given allotments of land on which they will live until they can sell out to white men. It is probable they will then go to Mexico or some other place where the paleface is not all-powerful.

Pioneer families labored to build their home and cultivate the land—two requirements of the Homestead Act.

Forward, ho! Covered wagons brought thousands of settlers to the plains to tame the wild and harness the free.

Of the great tract that is to be given away it is said by Government inspectors that eighty percent of the land is suitable for farming and that it will produce good crops. The rest of the land can be used for grazing purposes.

Across the range run the Wichita Mountains, which are said to contain gold and iron. Fifteen hundred mining claims can be entered under the general mining laws, and this fact has served to attract scores of miners. In all, the Government will be able to provide for thirty thousand people in the tract, as there must be at least five or six town sites laid out, and the town lots will be given away free. In every town there will be at least a thousand town lots.

The climate is about the same as that of North Carolina and Tennessee. There is some snow in winter, but it remains on the ground no longer than one day. The summers are hot, but a wind always rises at eventide, making the nights cool and pleasant.

Cotton, wheat and corn are the leading products, with fruit-raising fast coming to the fore.

(1901)

Edgar Watson Howe was born in 1853; he was six or seven years old when he made the trip described in a memoir written for the Post *in 1924. The journey ended near Bethany, Missouri, where Ed worked on the family farm until he was 12. He became, then, a printer, a newspaperman and finally the widely-known publisher of the* Atchison Daily Globe *as well as a frequent and widely acclaimed contributor to several national magazines.*

The Wagon and the West

Memoirs of E. W. Howe

My recollection begins with moving to a new country. I do not recall our talking about it before we started; as I look back at the past, the first thing I remember is a covered wagon standing in the yard, preparation for departure and neighbors calling to discuss the event in which I was so much interested.

We lived in a heavily wooded section in Indiana, and I often heard the men say the work of clearing the farms had made them prematurely old. That was mainly the excuse they gave for seeking the prairie country out West, hoping to grow up with it, although they complained a good deal of chills and fever.

I can recall a dozen or more of the families accompanying us, but I do not remember the houses they lived in, or our own very well; only that we were to start on a certain day and that I was impatient to get away to new scenes.

There were a good many loose horses and cattle to drive, unruly at first, though they soon became tractable; so we did not get far for the first camp. It was near the home of a man named Aaron Fair, who first heard of our adventure when he came to call on us. Learning where we were going and liking the prospect, he returned to his house, packed up, and, when we moved out next morning, was in our company. What he did with his farm I never knew. Probably he abandoned it, knowing that as good or better land could be had for nothing where we were going.

In a few days we met many other movers headed toward the West. Some of these joined us permanently, liking the talk of our men about the section they had selected. Three families starting with us joined other parties, and we saw no more of them.

I do not believe I had ever heard of a railroad until someone said in my presence we were in the vicinity of one. In a little while we were traveling beside it, and I was bothering everyone with questions. The wagon road ran below the railway, and before I could get satisfactory answers I heard a great rumble and saw the men suddenly jump out to hold the horses. Immediately the new thing, a railway train, appeared, and old Sam, one of our horses, made a scene. He was noted for being nervous and scary and made the most of the occasion; in his floundering he broke the tongue of the wagon, and it was necessary to replace it, causing a delay. I heard some of the men advise father to get rid of him.

"If I had a horse like that," one said, "I'd shoot him."

Not long after, we had trouble with the horse again, in crossing the Mississippi. But I was so much impressed with my first view of a river and a steamboat that I paid little attention to anything else. Finally we had to blindfold old Sam and lead him on and off the boat. The hissing steam frightened him, but not much more than it did me.

Back in the woods we came from, my father was preacher and farmer, and most of those following him to the West had been converted by his sermons and songs; for he was a great singer and able to read notes. They were different from the kind used in singing now, and we called them buckwheat notes. Prayer meetings were held every time we stopped for the night. Frequently these became animated and took on the nature of a revival. Once a big girl called Sarah Jane got religion. Bill Scott said, without meaning to be impious, that she came through, as they had been working on her before leaving Indiana. When Sarah Jane began shouting her mother soon joined her, and other women shouted because of the happiness of these two.

It always seemed to me that while the men encouraged the women to shout they did no shouting themselves. In my long experience with religious people I have never known a man to shout, but in the old days a service was rarely held that women did not engage in it. Some were more violent than others, but always it was a weird and impressive performance.

Several of the women in our group got together every evening and smoked clay pipes, which they

Scouts were invaluable to the wagon train. They located water and food sources; warned of imminent danger ahead.

lighted with coals from the campfires. At first they were timid about smoking in so great a company; I recall there was no smoking the first few days of the journey. Then a woman called Aunt Mahala did it, and several others joined her, one by one, until there was quite a gathering of smokers around her wagon. The children explained that their mothers smoked because they were troubled with neuralgia and tobacco was good for it.

I once tried smoking Aunt Mahala's pipe after she had laid it aside and became very sick. While in this condition someone reported the incident to my father, who came after me and gave me what we called a whaling. I saw him coming, trimming a switch, and understood what it meant, for whipping children was very common in that day.

The first compliment ever paid me was from my mother, who said I was a good-looking baby but had gotten bravely over it. The second came from my Aunt Beckie, who said I was smart; that when my father hit me the first lick I fell and screamed so loud he thought he was murdering me and soon quit, whereas my brother Jim sullenly took punishment, which caused the whip to be laid on all the harder.

We never made camp that some of the children were not whipped; frequently fathers and mothers led their children off, the children screaming, "I'll be good! I'll be good!"

Bill Scott, who I mentioned before, was a professional farm hand, and it was said he would never amount to anything else; but he was the most popular member of the party, and the most capable. He helped

Hard pressed to provide for their own, Indians seldom held captive the children of the white man.

the tired women with a gentleness and politeness I sincerely admired, since I had never seen anything of the kind before, and his sympathies were always with the children when they were imposed on. All the men were a little afraid of him in an argument or in wrestling.

One evening a party of Indians came along and camped near us. The leader was a white man married to an Indian woman. There was some objection to the Indians; I heard it said members of our party feared the Indians might steal some of us children. I had never before thought they worried that much about us.

The white man with an Indian family somehow heard of the talk and said there needn't be any worry on that score; that we could have some of his children, and welcome, if we wanted them. Later he talked disagreeably, and it was Bill Scott who told him to do less of it. The man looked Bill over carefully and thought it best to adopt the suggestion. The Indians left next morning without taking any of us.

Another mover, named Alfred Burt, was noted because he had been the subject of an adventure. In cleaning out a well the rock wall caved in, covering him to a depth of many feet. It was Bill Scott who took charge of the rescue party and performed miracles of hard work. The Burts were our nearest neighbors in Indiana, and I had stood about the well several hours while the men were working at the rescue.

Alfred Burt was unusual in another respect: His wagon was pulled by a yoke of oxen, and he managed to keep up with us. The men said he got along well because he had little in his wagon, as he had no children; all the others had their weapons loaded with them.

The Lantises had nine, and one of them, a boy named Dan, died on the way. He was buried in a graveyard we passed, and we sang a hymn beginning "Hark from the tomb a doleful sound" as we committed his body to the grave. I can still sing that hymn, also, and make dogs howl, it is so sad. The Lantises went on with us, but Mrs. Lantis cried most of the time. In a few days she induced her husband to go back to the vicinity of her son's grave and take up land. We never saw them again.

Mrs. Alfred Burt was a singer, as was my father, and these two led the frequent song services.

Soon after we started from Indiana we were joined on the road by a man named Lang, who had neither wife nor children. He said he had been a widower five years—which was unusual, as widowers I had known married in two or three months. One in our neighborhood married in two weeks giving as excuse that he had several little children needing attention. The women were not very well satisifed, but seemed to forgive him. Anyway he was with our party and about as well thought of as anyone.

The Koerner prairie woman—a blend of back East femininity and out West stoicism. A picture of quiet strength.

Lang was a jolly man, but many thought he overdid it. He associated with the women and girls a good deal but not as unobjectionably as did Bill Scott, the bachelor, who was a help to them rather than a burden. Lang tried to be so popular that he would be invited to eat his meals at other campfires to avoid cooking himself, but he failed and was compelled to do his own. He made a good deal of the Burts, as he was a singer, and seemed to have a notion he was as clever at it as my father. He spent a good deal of time with Mrs. Burt, practicing songs he knew but which were new to us.

I awoke one morning to find most of the men gone and an air of intense excitement about the camp. My mother was over at another wagon, talking with a group of women, and breakfast was late. But when I learned the particulars I soon forgot I was hungry. Lang and Mrs. Alfred Burt had disappeared during the night, and the men had gone after them.

From the big boys, and by piecing bits together here and there, I learned that at midnight Lang had offered to watch the stock alone until daylight. Sometime later he had hitched up his team and driven quietly away

Fording a stream could mean trouble for the wagon train if there were swift currents, high waters or muddy shores.

with Mrs. Burt. When the men began getting up in the morning they made the discovery and, saddling their horses, galloped away furiously.

About sundown they returned with the runaways. Someone had hit Lang, for his face was puffy and discolored, and I heard my father did it, although he was a religious man and devoted to the gentle art of music.

Alfred Burt took his wife back, but Bill Scott had charge of Lang. After the men had eaten supper the adults met and discussed the affair. They at first drove

me away, but I was so persistent, and the excitement at the meeting became so great, that at last they paid no attention to me.

I know little about the affair now except that both Lang and Mrs. Burt remained with us thereafter, about as before, although neither was permitted to attend the religious services. Later the movers built a church at their last camp on Big Creek, but the runaways were never permitted to enter its doors. Lang afterward married the big girl we called Sarah Jane and, when I left the party long ago, seemed to be getting along about as well as anyone.

One of the movers had been a blacksmith in Indiana and intended pursuing the same calling in the new country. He had his forge along and every night when we stopped shod horses or did such other work as was necessary. I have forgotten this man's name but recall that his wife bossed him—the first case of the kind I had ever known. All the other wives were submissive, overworked, frightened and not very strong, while several of the men were still hearty with second and third wives. I supposed all wives were submissive to husbands until I knew the blacksmith's family. The blacksmith was a poor collector, and his wife abused him a good deal for his fault in the presence of those who owed him money. She was not only fearless of her husband but had a contempt for other men, one of whom I once heard say, "If I had that woman I'd wring her neck."

The other men and boys, when meals were ready, sat down first and the women waited on them, but the blacksmith's wife had different notions.

I can still remember what we had to eat on the way; mainly pork meat in some form, cured in Indiana before we started, and corn bread. The cooking was done in huge iron skillets we called spiders, with tops. Live coals from the fire were placed on the covers. A good many supplies were bought on the way, including corn, which the children sometimes roasted, ground in coffee mills and ate with milk. Nearly every family had brought cows along, which were milked morning and evening. We also had chickens and ducks, and these were released from their coops in the evening to run about and feed. At the proper time every fowl went back to its coop to roost, and the door was closed. One woman had several geese, and I recall these chasing me and hissing. We occasionally encountered a water mill on the way, where we bought meal. A frequent sight on the road was a boy on horseback going to mill with a bag of corn behind him.

Every night the cows and horses were herded by two men until midnight, when they came in for two others. All the men took turns at this, and I remembered their saying certain horses and cows were natural vagrants and would stray off unless closely watched, while the others remained contentedly near camp.

We were on the road so long it seemed we would go on forever, but one day

Horseshoes, more than luck to the smith; a livelihood.

we stopped, and father said we had reached the end of the journey. The country was rolling prairie, with woods in the distance.

For several days the men were away, to see about the land, and I believe the women enjoyed their absence as much as the children did.

When the men returned they were more surly than usual; apparently they had been having trouble in making their locations and having disagreements. There was no prayer meeting that night. Being a preacher, father probably thought that much was expected of him, in spite of the way he had been treated by his companions at the land office. I heard him grumble a good deal about this to my mother but never knew the details.

Next morning we couldn't hitch up and proceed on our way, so with less to do than ever before we went to work and contributed what was to be our small share to the development of the West. (1924)

From the Big Woods to Plum Creek

Rose Wilder Lane,

as told her by her mother, Laura Ingalls Wilder

As a child, Rose Wilder begged her mother to tell, over and over again, the story of her parents and how they traveled West by covered wagon. The mother was, of course, Laura Ingalls Wilder, and she later told the story in the enormously popular "Little House" books that inspired the successful television series. The excerpt that follows is from a fictionalized version of the story that Rose wrote for the Post *in 1932. The original title was "Let the Hurricane Roar"; the original illustrations were by W. H. D. Koerner.*

While they were children playing together, they said they would be married as soon as they were old enough, and when they were old enough they married. Charles liked to remind her that he had never asked her to marry him; he liked to see her smile sedately, as she always smiled at his teasing.

She was a quiet person. When she was a little girl she was often asked if the cat had got her tongue. Even with   Charles she had a way of saying nothing

in words. Her eyes, which could not lie, told what she felt. Before she smiled, a shadowy dimple quivered in one cheek. Her face was quiet under smooth wings of hair, her movements gentle and deft. In her heart she never quite lost the wonder that she, quiet, shy and not very pretty, had won such a man. He was laughing and bold, a daring hunter, a dancer, fiddler and fighter.

She thought of him as he was on summer Sunday afternoons when his family was spending the day with hers. Perhaps other neighbors were there, too.

The old men sat on the bench against the shady side of the log house, talking slowly, with chuckles and long pauses. Their sons went out to look at the calf and pigs. Children ran about, climbing the rail fence, raiding the wild blackberry thickets. The babies slept on a faded quilt in the shade of the oak, and near them the women rested on benches brought from the house. Charles' grandmother swayed in the hickory rocker that bumped over the uneven ground. Everything in the clearing was drowsy till Charles sat down on a stump and tuned his fiddle.

His favorite hymn always lifted him to his feet. His chin left the fiddle, he shook back his thick brown hair. His voice rang out above all the other voices; it led the defiant, triumphant song that surged across the stumpy fields and echoed into the vast, unconquered forest:

Let the hurricane roar!
It will the sooner be o'er!
We'll weather the blast, and land at last,
On Canaan's happy shore!

Many settlers had come to the settlement in the Big Woods while Charles and Caroline were growing up. When they married there was little good land left. Farther west, the country was not yet settled and the land was said to be rich and level, and without forests. So they went west.

Charles' father was an open-handed man and he had six sons younger than Charles; he could afford to be generous. Charles was not yet 19. His labor belonged to his father until he was 21. But his father gave him his time—a free gift of more than two years. To cap this, for good measure heaped up and running over, he gave Charles the team and wagon he would have earned by work-ing till he was 21.

Caroline's parents gave her two blankets, two goose-feath-er pillows, and cooking pot and pan and skillet. They gave her a ham, a cheese, two molds of maple sugar and Tennyson's *Poems* beautifully bound in green and gilt, with steel engravings. She had the patchwork quilts she had pieced. Charles had his fiddle and his gun. Their families together sent East for their Bible, and the circuit rider wrote their marriage certificate on the page provided for it. The pages for Births and Deaths were still blank, waiting to be written upon. So, well provided for, they set out to the West.

Priceless presents for westward bound newlyweds—a team of horses, complete with wagon, and basic provisions.

At first Caroline was sad because she was leaving her family forever. She ached for the busy life with her mother and sisters in the log cabin, for her father's coming home from work or hunting, even for the oak tree by the door and the path to the spring. But these memories soon ceased to hurt her, in her happiness with Charles.

They could never decide which was best—the fresh mornings when the first rays of the sun found Caroline packing the washed dishes and Charles whistling while he hitched up the team; or varied days of traveling westward on unknown roads; or evenings by the fire. Charles played his fiddle while the horses grazed and stars or moon shone overhead and the night air was sweet. Or they sat cozily together with the firelight on their faces, and talked about the things they had seen that day and the home they would have in the West. Then Caroline banked the fire while Charles tied the horses safe for the night, and they went to bed in the wagon.

Every day Charles shot game. When they needed flour and tea and sugar, they camped at some settlement while he worked for supplies. Whenever he had money, he brought her a present; once a little box covered with tiny shells, a mirror set in the lid; and once 15 yards of calico for a dress she didn't really need. She scolded him, for she was thrifty, but she never cured him of bringing her presents. He liked to see the shining in her eyes.

Late that summer they reached the western prairie and Charles got a job, teaming on the railroad. They were going to have a baby, and he wanted to earn money. The homestead could wait, he said; he would look around for one, and meantime she must stay in the railroad camp.

The long railroad embankment was being pushed westward. Scores of men and teams were working on it, raising a low smoke of dust under the enormous sky. The camp was small on the immense plain, where there was nothing but miles of wild grass blowing in the wind.

The bunkhouse, the cookhouse and the company store were all of raw new lumber. The contractor's wife had a little frame shanty, and so did her sister who ran the cookhouse, but they were crowded and Caroline did not want to stay in them. Charles built her a sod shanty. He cut the strips of tough sod and she helped him to lay up the walls and stretch the canvas wagon top over them. A thatch of slough grass kept out the heat of the sun. In two days the house was done, neat and cool and all her own. Charles was hauling supplies to the new camp, 20 miles west. Every second night he was away from her, and she was lonely. She could not like Mrs. Baker or her sister. They were coarse, blowzy women, much older than she. She talked more to their children, who ran about bare-legged and brown, whooping and racing their bare-backed ponies over the prairie.

On nights when Charles was away, she lay awake a long time. A distant wolf howled. A coyote prowled softly around the shanty. The company store was noisy with boots and the rough voices of men drinking and gambling. A lonely voice went by, singing:

I've been working on the railroad,
All the livelong day;
I've been working on the railroad,
To pass the time away.

Charles had given her a gun and she was never afraid. But she wanted Charles to be there. The loneliness was hard to endure. Her hands and face were brown as an Indian's from the prairie wind and sun. When she unpinned the collar of her basque, it was odd to see the brown face on the milk-white neck. Charles teased her: "Come here, squaw! Give me a kiss. Oh, little squaw, little squaw, your baby's going to be a papoose!"

She thought about this, sitting on his knee. "Well," she said soberly, "it's your baby, too."

She never understood his shout of amusement when she said something plainly true, like that. But she knew his laughter was part of his loving her.

In September the winds were edged with cold and all day long the gray sky resounded to the signal calls of

Life on the road: traveling and shooting game by day; playing the fiddle and talking in the firelight by night.

wild birds flying south. The men worked sullenly in cold winds and dust. All their wages had gone back to the company store and now the camps were closing; there would be no more work till next year. In the camp farther west there were riots about wages; men were killed. But Caroline knew that Charles could take care of himself. He had earned money enough for the winter's supplies and for tools and seed, and he had found a homestead. His blue eyes sparkled when he told her. There was already a dugout and barn, and 50 acres of the sod were broken. Another man had taken the land and done all that work, yet he was giving up, he was going back East. He said he could not stand another winter of loneliness.

Charles asked, "Would it be too lonesome for you, Caroline? There won't be another human being within 30, 40 miles."

"You wouldn't have to go away?"

"No, I'd be there, but—"

He did not finish the sentence, so she said, "No, I won't be lonesome."

In the middle of the night Charles started to the Land Office, to get that homestead before anyone else. He was not yet 20, but he would say he was 21; the government would never know the difference. Caroline listened to the jolting of his wagon going away in the dark. It was 30 miles to the Land Office.

Three days went by. The sun had set; the sky was pale, cold yellow, flushed with pink all around the rim of the horizon, when Caroline heard the rattle of the wagon, far away. Charles was jubilantly singing. She could hear only the tune, but she knew the words:

Come to this country and don't you feel alarm,
For Uncle Sam is rich enough to give us all a farm!

She knew he had the papers. In five years they would own their land.

Work stopped in the camps. Under the lines of wild birds flying south, a stream of men was going east. In wagons, on horseback, on foot, they were going back to the settled country. The bunkhouse was empty and the cookhouse closed. In the chill wind Caroline helped Charles pack supplies and take the canvas wagon top from the sod shanty. They slept in the wagon that night, and next morning Charles hitched up the horses and they started west. The camp was dark. Only the Bakers were busy with lanterns, loading the last of the

An old photo captures a moment of idleness, rare in a setting where hard work is obviously the rule of the day.

company goods into their wagons headed east. Charles stopped in front of the store to say good-bye. Mrs. Baker was angry when she heard that Charles and Caroline were not going out for the winter. She was a big, coarse woman, who cut her hair like a man's and did not wear corsets. She faced Charles, hands on hips.

"That child, in her condition!" she said. "You want to kill her?"

Her blunt talk frightened Charles. He had not supposed it was so dangerous for a woman to have a baby, but now he was ready to abandon everything and take Caroline east. He agreed that she must have neighbor women with her. But Caroline thought of the homestead. She knew that claim jumpers would get it; they might kill Charles when he came back to it in the spring.

The dugout was cozy while winds howled and the deep snow moved in drifts over the land. On clear days Charles went out with his gun and came back with meat and furs. Caroline scrubbed and baked and washed and ironed and cooked. On days when the blizzards came shrieking from the northwest, Charles groped his way only to the barn and back. He had stretched a rope from the top of the path to the barn door, so he would not lose his way in the blinding storms, but Caroline was uneasy until he came back safe.

Yet those days were best of all. Charles cleaned his gun, oiled his boots, twisted slough hay for the fire. From two packing boxes he made a cradle. He scraped the wood carefully with a bit of broken lamp chimney, till it was as smooth as his hand, and on the headboard he carved two birds and a nest. The place was gay with his whistling while he worked. Caroline saved her mending and sewing for these stormy days. She worked quietly, smiling to herself. The lamplight was cheerful, the stove gave out its heat and the good smell of cooking. Then Charles took his fiddle from its box; he played and sang, keeping time with a patting foot. Those were festive days. On Sundays they did not work, and Charles played only hymns. It was splendid to see and hear him, roaring out his favorite to the wind that howled in the stovepipe. Then Caroline read to him. Charles was a slow reader, but he liked to listen while Caroline read aloud. She read the Bible, and she read Tennyson's *Poems*. That winter she read the green-and-gilt book from cover to cover. It made their life even more rich and beautiful.

February was clear; the cold was so intense that the air seemed glittering ice, and the silent world was buried in snow. Caroline was heavy now and clumsy, and her breath was short. Though the weather was good for hunting, Charles went only to the barn and back; he would not leave her long alone. Sometimes, even when he was there, Caroline heard the silence and was afraid. The silence of those miles of snow untouched by any trace of human beings, marked only by the inhuman winds and the paws

The miracle of birth was especially wondrous on the prairie, where help was often miles, even days, away.

of wild animals, was without enmity or pity. Its indifference was more cruel than hate.

She tried to remember all she had heard about childbirth; it was very little. She did not let Charles guess how much she wanted her mother.

The pain began early one afternoon. She had set a batch of bread; she moved the pan nearer the stove so that the dough would rise more quickly. Charles must have food while she was unable to cook. He was twisting hay for fuel, whistling while he twisted, doubled, knotted the long strands into firm sticks, and she was able to knead the bread and mold it into loaves before he saw her face.

She had known the pain would be bad and was resolved to make no outcry. She would not make it harder for Charles. Indian women bore their babies silently.

That night was very long. She lay in the bunk and smiled at Charles whenever she could. Even worse than the pain was the terror. Her courage seemed so small against the implacable indifference that possessed her body. Desperately she clung to Charles, but even Charles was helpless. She did not scream. In the moments when she was herself again, she was glad and a little proud that she had not screamed. Charles wiped the sweat from her face. She smiled at him and spoke happily about the baby.

Several times she asked in surprise, "Isn't it morning yet?"

Then everything became confused. Daylight and darkness were mixed. She heard shrieks and knew they were hers; she could not stop them. Even Charles was gone. There was nothing anywhere but unbearable agony. She herself was ebbing, going—a last little atom fighting, failing—

The baby was born in the morning of the second day. For a long time she knew that she was lying under eyelids too heavy to lift. She lifted them at last and saw Charles' face. Tears of pity came into her eyes. Her voice had no sound.

He bent lower, and she whispered in his ear, "How—is—the—papoose?"

She wanted to make him smile. When he sobbed, she thought the baby was dead. The tears ran from her eyes. But Charles sobbed, "He's all right. Oh, Caroline, Caroline—"

The baby had been born on her seventeenth birthday, like a present. Caroline noticed this when Charles was writing the baby's name and the date on the blank page for Births in their Bible. She hoped the baby would be like Charles, but she was glad he had been born on her own birthday.

They named him Charles John. He was a fat, healthy baby, and almost never cried. Charles teased him, tickled him, rumpled and tossed him. In fact, the baby first laughed at sight of Charles. Caroline washed his clothes every day and bathed him in snow water heated on the stove. When she sat holding him while he nursed, her happiness almost frightened her; it seemed too great to keep. (1932)

W.H.D. Koerner Studio, Whitney Gallery of Western Art, Cody, Wyoming

Charles John didn't merely add to his parents' happiness with one another—he multiplied it many times over.

The Man Who Was Grateful

A Story by David Lamson

Mother wanted to call on the Hoogsteens when they first came to our country and took up a homestead a little way down the road from ours, but my father would not let her.

"You wait," he said. "Don't be in such a rush to make friends with everybody that comes along. Wait till we know more about them."

"It's just common courtesy to stop by and say how-do, somebody just moved in," mother said. "We don't have to make friends if we don't want to. You're so standoffish, Joe, I don't know what ails you."

"Well, I don't know what ails you, either, the way you take up with new people. One week you'll be makin' soft soap together, and the next you can't say mean enough about 'em."

"Why, Joe Plimpton, I don't either!"

"No? What about Mrs. Finley, then?"

"Well, her!" Mother sniffed scornfully, the way you do when you can't think of any good answer, and went out in the kitchen and slammed the door.

So we did not call on the Hoogsteens, and did not see much of them until the day, two or three months later, when Mrs. Hoogsteen came hurrying up to our house carrying this dog, this fox terrier they had brought with them from Michigan. His name was Poodles, and he was a nervous, yelpy little brute, but there was not much yelp left in him now, because he had found a porcupine in the woods and collected a faceful of quills. And Mr. Hoogsteen was away from home, so his wife came to us for help.

Mrs. Hoogsteen seemed very distressed over what had happened to Poodles. She was half crying, and she kept saying, "Will he die, huh? You think he will die, no?" The Hoogsteens had no children, and they were un-

derstandably fond of their little Poodles.

Father assured her that Poodles would be as good as new in half an hour—porcupine quills won't kill a dog, unless they are left to work their way in to a vital spot. We finally got the dog away from her, and father and I went down to the blacksmith shed with him while mother took Mrs. Hoogsteen in the house to console her. I held Poodles, and father went to work with the pliers. The pup seemed to know he'd made a fool of himself; he held right still and let father twitch the quills out one by one, whimpering softly over the worst ones. Our own dog, Jeff, who went through life convinced that some day he'd find a porcupine he could whip, and so had to be dequilled two or three times a year, looked on sympathetically. When we finished and put Poodles down, Jeff came over and licked his face for him.

Mrs. Hoogsteen stayed on an hour or so after father and I went back to work on the roof of the hay shed.

That night mother had a new kind of dried-apple cake for supper, which she said Mrs. Hoogsteen had told her how to make. Father gave her a look.

"So," he said. "At it already, huh?"

Mother said, "I don't know what you're talking about. Anyway, Mrs. Hoogsteen is a real nice woman,

and it's a pleasure to see a new face once in a while. I declare, anybody'd think you was practicing up to be a hermit, the way you act."

"Never mind how I act. I just don't like to have strangers livin' right in my pocket, is all."

And that was the whole size of it. Father was a friendly enough man, really, and certainly he did not dislike the Hoogsteens, but he resented the idea of having anyone living within a quarter mile of us. When we first came to Northern Alberta our nearest neighbor lived three miles away, and we could go for weeks at a time without seeing anyone but our own folks, unless we chose. That suited father just fine. He said it gave him room to move in, and quiet to hear himself think. He said he felt sorry for anyone who was such bad company for himself he had to have other folks around all the time. When the country began to settle up and they cut the road through to Moose Creek settlement past our place, he used to talk about moving on farther north, where things weren't so crowded.

But father was a polite man, and he gave the Hoogsteens a friendly welcome when they came to the door on the next Sunday. Mrs. Hoogsteen was all dressed up in a red velvet jacket and a black straw hat with a big bunch of flowers sticking up on it; and Mr. Hoogsteen, who was about half her size and had long yellow mustaches, wore a blue serge suit and a high celluloid collar with a red-and-green necktie clipped to it. A big yellow mixing bowl was clasped in his arms. The moment father opened the door, Mr. Hoogsteen began making a speech in a booming, singsong voice surprisingly deep for so small a man.

"I give you good day, Mr. Plimpton," he said. "Excuse us, please, that we have you disturbed once; we come to make thanks for helping us by our little dog with the porcupine quills. That was good, kind thing to do, and we thank you very much yet, so here is a little somet'ing, a little bowl sauerkraut my wife has made already, we bring it to you, we hope you like it, oh, yes, thank you!"

That was something of the way he put his words together, as I remember it, but nothing like the way it sounded. Father had been asleep in his armchair when they knocked at the door, and he was more or less overwhelmed by it all. He stood there blinking at the bowl of sauerkraut thrust into his hands, trying to decide which of Mr. Hoogsteen's remarks he ought to answer first.

He said, "Why, that's all right. You're welcome. I mean, thanks very much. Uh—pup get along all right, did he?"

Mrs. Hoogsteen beamed and nodded. "Oh-h, yes, fine—like you say, just so good as new already!"

Father looked at the bowl he was holding. "Sauerkraut, eh? Say, that's mighty nice of you. Nothin' I like better than a good mess o' kraut."

Suddenly he remembered his manners, and pushed at the door with his elbow. "Here now, what's the matter with me, keepin' you standing out there? Come in, come in!...Bub, take this bowl...Where's your mother?...Amy!...Oh, there you are. Here's the Hoogsteens come to see us."

Mother came in, drying her hands on her apron and smiling at the Hoogsteens. She said, "I'm real glad to see you. Come right in and have a chair."

But they would not come in. Standing on the doorstep, his wife nodding and smiling over his head, Mr. Hoogsteen solemnly repeated, word for word, his little speech of gratitude, including that about the sauerkraut. At the end he said abruptly, "We go now. Good-by....Come, Katy."

He wheeled and marched away, down the driveway. Mrs. Hoogsteen lingered long enough to say gently, "The sauerkraut. It is the same like we used to make it once, when I was little girl in Michigan. I hope you like it, yes."

"Oh, we will," said mother. "I do wish you'd come in a minute."

Mrs. Hoogsteen said, "You will come see us maybe, no? Yes! Good-by now."

Her husband was almost at the gate; he did not wait for her, nor did she try to overtake him. They walked down the road in that order, a dozen yards apart. And yet, watching them, you had no feeling of any antagonism between them, nor even of indifference. They had somehow a code and an understanding of their own, which they followed with a direct simplicity.

Their refusal to enter our house, which might have been insulting in another, was of the same nature. But father was puzzled by it. He said, "Say, what's the matter with them, anyway? Why wouldn't they come in, long as they was here?"

Mother took the bowl of kraut out of my hands. "Because we've never been to see them, of course!" she said crisply. "What do you expect? They're not going to force themselves on us when we're so high and mighty. Three, going on four months, and we've never been a-near!"

Father said, "Um-m," and rubbed his chin thoughtfully. "Well, anyhow, it was nice of 'em to bring us that kraut. I been hungry for some. Why don't you ever make sauerkraut any more, Amy?"

Mother banged the bowl down on the table. "Joe Plimpton, I like that! What did you tell me, the very last time I made it?"

"Tell you?" said father. "Why, let's see——"

"You said you never wanted to see another bit of sauerkraut as long as you lived! Your very words!"

"Oh," said father. "Did I? Funny, I'd forgotten. Had a little too much of it, probably. You know I always did like kraut."

Mother had taken the cover off the bowl and was looking in it. She said, "You can eat this, then. All of it, all by yourself."

"Now, Amy, no need to——"

"Look at it," said mother.

Father bent over the bowl, and sniffed at it. "Caraway seed!" he exclaimed. He made a face. "Gosh darn the luck, what'd she want to do that for?"

Mother giggled, and father's face got red. He said, "Caraway seed!" in a disgusted voice. He sat down and pulled his shoes on, and picked up the bowl and marched out of the house with it. I saw him stop at the tool shed and pick up a shovel, and go on around the corner of the barn.

I said, "What's he going to do with it, ma?"

"Bury it, I guess. Your father never could abide anything with spice in it." She looked at me sharply. "And if you know what's good for you, young man,

you won't talk about sauerkraut for a while where he can hear you."

She giggled again. "Your father's been hurt in his dignity," she said, "and that's more'n any man can stand."

Of course, then we had to return their visit, and take back the bowl, and the bowl had to have something in it. Saturday was baking day, so on the next Sunday mother wrapped up two loaves of fresh bread and we went down there.

On the way father said to me, "Look here, Bub, just because we don't like caraway seed is no reason for hurtin' Mrs. Hoogsteen's feelings. That was first-class sauerkraut—if you happen to like it that way—and we're goin' to be polite about it and tell her so. And if you go to actin' funny, or talkin' out of turn, I'll larrup you good!"

I said, "Yes, sir!" and tried to catch mother's eye,

Not sharing the sentiment, the outsider may regard the dish "made like mother used to make it" with skepticism.

but she would not look at me. Father must have known we were both laughing inside, because he acted as if he would have liked to pitch into us; but he didn't have any excuse.

Sure enough, Mrs. Hoogsteen made a great fuss over the bread, admiring it and praising it, so, naturally, someone had to praise up her sauerkraut the same way. Father looked over at mother and frowned and nodded, but she just smiled at him, so he had to do it all. I will say he did a good job. He sounded really enthusiastic. He tried to bring mother into it by asking her if it wasn't true, all he had said.

"Oh, yes, indeed," said mother. "Joe's a great hand for sauerkraut. In fact, he took care of that whole bowl of it, all by himself. The rest of us didn't get even a taste!"

Mrs. Hoogsteen looked pleased and startled, and then she gave mother and me a sympathetic look, as if she were thinking father was a greedy fellow. Father didn't stay in the house long after that. He went outside with Mr. Hoogsteen to look around the place.

He seemed to warm up to Mr. Hoogsteen when he saw how much work the man had done. The buildings weren't much—a one-room log cabin chinked with mud, and a lean-to shed for their one horse—but he had a couple of acres dug up and into vegetables for winter, and he was clearing more land as fast as he could. He was cutting the trees off close to the ground—he had small stuff mostly on his place, poplar and a few spruce—and piling the poles for fence rails and burning the brush. Poplar stumps rot quickly; in two or three years he would be able to plow out most of them. Meanwhile he would plow around them the best he could, and they were cut low enough for a mowing machine to go over them.

This was the same method of clearing my father used, so, naturally, he was pleased with Mr. Hoogsteen. He told Mr. Hoogsteen all about building a root cellar that would be frostproof even in sixty-below-zero weather, and about the best crops for a first planting on new land. Mr. Hoogsteen said little until it was time for us to go. Then he had over all about father's kindness to Poodles, and Mrs. Hoogsteen brought out another bowl of sauerkraut, made with caraway seed, for us to take home with us.

Most homesteaders put their houses as close to the road as they could, but Mr. Hoogsteen had built quite a way back, on the far side of a poplar ridge. By September he had a long, narrow clearing cut through to the road, between ten and fifteen acres. In that month some people east of town sold out at auction, and the Hoogsteens bid in two more horses—old, but

sound and strong—a wagon, a breaking plow and a disk harrow, besides some other odds and ends.

He went to work at once with his three horses, breaking his cleared land in preparation for a second plowing the next spring. Mrs. Hoogsteen helped him with the breaking, driving the team while he held the plow. We saw them at it when we drove uptown, past their place. They were having a hard time of it; holding down a breaking plow in stump land is no job for a little man, especially if he is using horses instead of oxen. Horses try to go too fast, and they get excited and start lunging and pulley-hauling when the plow hangs up on a root, as it frequently does.

Father said something of this to Mr. Hoogsteen when we stopped to talk for a minute. Hoogsteen did not answer him for so long a time that father grew uncomfortable under his bleak, remote gaze.

At last he said, "In Michigan on my father's farm always there were horses. Only horses. Yes. Good-by now.... Katy, say 'Giddup' once."

"Giddup!" said Katy briskly to the horses, and to father, "You folks come see us by 'm by, no?"

The aroma of fresh-baked bread is something persons of all ages and backgrounds can appreciate.

Opportunities for neighborly visits were few and far between, as were the homes and the moments of leisure.

They went floundering down the furrow, leaving father looking uneasy. He had meant his remark about horses and oxen as a general comment, but Mr. Hoogsteen seemed to have taken it personally as a criticism and an interference.

They got the land turned over, after a fashion, and some days later when we passed that way we saw Mr. Hoogsteen working alone, the three horses hooked to his disk harrow. He was riding the disk, driving with one hand and clinging to the seat with the other, and having trouble staying on. Whenever the disk ran over a stump the steel blades cut into the wood and then sprang loose suddenly, causing the whole machine to buck like a bronco. I thought it a comical sight, but father was frowning.

"He hadn't ought to ride that thing," he said. "He'll hurt his fool self." He tightened the lines as if he meant to stop and speak to Mr. Hoogsteen, but he thought better of it—remembering, perhaps, the matter of the oxen—and we went on to town.

On our way home we looked for Mr. Hoogsteen, but he was not in sight. The team was standing in the field well back from the road, half hidden behind a rise of land. Father eyed them for a moment, and then stood up in the wagon, trying to see over the hill, but only the backs of the horses were visible. The horse on the off-side had his head turned back, apparently watching something on the ground behind him; the near horse tossed his head and seemed to paw restlessly.

I said "What's the matter?" seeing father's mouth draw up and his eyes narrow, but he didn't answer me. He stopped our team and threw me the lines and leaped out of the wagon.

"Take a turn on the hub," he called, "and come a-runnin'!"

He ran as fast as he could across the field toward the Hoogsteen horses. I fastened the lines to the wheel, so they would tighten if the team moved forward, and followed him. When the horses raised their heads and pricked their ears toward him, he stopped running and walked quietly toward them, circling a little to approach them from the front.

As he neared the top of the rise, moving ever more slowly, he began to talk to them: "Whoa, boys, easy now, so, so. . . .Bub, don't you scare 'em, keep in back o' me. . . .Whoa, boys, whoa there——"

Mr. Hoogsteen lay on the ground behind the horses, pinned down by the weight of the disk on his legs. He lay perfectly still, watching us. The horse on the off-side snorted and tossed his head, rolling his eyes at us; father stopped in his tracks and stood motionless, talking, talking, until the animal's head dropped. He moved forward again, his hand out, soothing them with his voice. He had hold of the bits. "Get a hold here, Bub. Hold 'em steady now. . . .You cut any, Hoogsteen?"

"No. I think no."

Father braced his legs and took hold of the disk axle and lifted mightily. Hoogsteen wriggled clear and sat on the ground, rubbing his numbed legs and moaning to himself. He had been in a bad spot. The disk had bucked over a hidden stump and thrown him forward, and had run up on his legs halfway to the knees before the team stopped in response to his shout. Luckily he was wearing high laced boots, which kept the sharp steel plates from cutting his legs.

He had clung to the lines, but they weren't much use to him. He could not back the disk, which had no tongue; if the team had drawn it forward, the blades would have torn him to pieces. Disk plates are mounted in series of two axles, set at an angle to each other, forcing the blades to cut deep into the soil.

So he had lain there, afraid to call out for fear of frightening the horses, for upward of half an hour, until my father came along.

Father took no great credit to himself for having rescued Hoogsteen from beneath the disk, nor was he much impressed by the accident itself. Farmers deal with edged tools, heavy weights and brute creatures, all potentially deadly, singly or in combination. The risk of injury is always present, especially in a frontier country where tools and methods are often makeshift. They take for granted the casual hazards and the narrow escapes as a part of their living.

But Mr. Hoogsteen took a serious view of the mishap—and incidentally, made no further attempt to ride the disk, although, as he assured us, on his father's farm in Michigan, where there were no stumps, it had been his invariable habit to do so. Convinced that he owed his life to father, he set himself to pay the debt. The warm flood of his gratitude foamed over us without ceasing; and father, after his first embarrassment, grew daily more harried and grim.

They brought us gifts, especially food. Mrs. Hoogsteen baked bread, cakes and cookies in great variety, and in nearly all of them she mixed quantities of caraway seeds. She believed that my father was especially fond of caraway seeds, and each new gift made it more impossible to explain that she was mistaken in this—for then she would have understood that her earlier offerings had not been enjoyed, and she would have been unhappy.

She made great dishes of hasenpfeffer for us; father hated spiced meats, and rabbits were so numerous that we were all sick of the sight of them. To say that a man ate rabbit was an insult in our country.

To father's mind, vegetables and fruits had a definite place in the scheme of things and were to be kept separate. Mrs. Hoogsteen made preserves out of turnips, beets and radishes, and pickles out of dried prunes.

Clearing the land was a matter of teamwork, as shown here, where man and his beasts team up against Nature.

A neighbor pitching in could help get the job done quicker—but seldom could he be spared from his own place.

And, always, there was caraway seed sauerkraut.

The dishes in which these gifts were brought to us could not be sent back empty. During that autumn I wore a path to the Hoogsteen cabin, and it seemed to me that Mrs. Hoogsteen spent all her time cooking for us, and mother spent all her time cooking for the Hoogsteens. Mrs. Hoogsteen worked a table runner for mother. Mother crocheted a lace collar for Mrs. Hoogsteen. Mrs. Hoogsteen knitted father a pair of mittens, in many bright colors and a chain-lightning pattern, and followed this up with a scarf to match. Father disliked having his neck bundled up, and refused to submit to any sort of muffler, but he wore Mrs. Hoogsteen's scarf when we called on them. They paid us a visit about once a week, and each visit had to be returned by us.

These were the formal, social calls. In addition, Mr. Hoogsteen came to our place two or three times each week to work for us. He seemed to feel that father had acquired a right to his services as well as his goods. Father, an intense libertarian, found this idea repugnant. At first he tried to argue with Mr. Hoogsteen.

"It's mighty fine of you to want to help, and all that," he said, "but the fact is right now there's nothin' Bub and me can't handle between us. Your own place needs all your time, I should think."

Mr. Hoogsteen stared at him with mournful stubbornness. "What would be happen to my place already except for what you have done?" he demanded. "Where would be my Katy if you didn't save me, huh?"

Father reddened unhappily. "Shucks, that was nothin'. Anyway, we been all over that——"

"I think it was not nothing. I think it was something. I am grateful feller, me. You help me from getting killed, I help you with working yet. You are good, kind——"

Father could not stand that kind of talk. "All right, all right," he said hastily. "Mighty kind of you. Not that it's necessary, but——Oh, well!"

So Mr. Hoogsteen helped us harvest and store the root crops, and helped us bring in the marsh hay from the upper end of the slough, for bedding, and helped us mend fence lines against the winter. When there was nothing else to be done, he chopped wood for us.

Thus we were driven into an involuntary change of work with him—for the work, like the food, had to be

A well-kept fire within can warm in an instant the bleakness of stark-looking trees and an isolated dwelling.

returned in kind, to make it even. Changing work was common practice in a country where no one had money for hired men and there were no hired men to be had anyway. But this situation was different, because we were under the constant obligation to help Mr. Hoogsteen. It was the obligation, the compulsion, that galled father.

Usually, father was a cheerful worker, whistling and singing and teasing me, and sometimes talking to me of all this and that, as if I were a man, and never crowding the work unless it was something that had to be done in a hurry. But now, with a third person there, unwanted, he was silent and cranky, and he drove at the job all the time. It was like working for wages, and no comfort in it.

In February father decided he would put up ice to be used the next summer—although mother said it was

nonsense, with our well water freezing cold all summer long and the ground never thawing under the moss on the north side of fir thickets. But father wanted ice to make ice cream.

He built a crib in back of the granary—Mr. Hoogsteen helped us—and he worked the next day in the blacksmith shed, making a big pair of tongs with which to haul the blocks out of the creek by horse power. We worked alone doing this; I ran the bellows on the forge for him, and it was like old times, with father whistling and cheerful.

We made an early start for Moose Creek, but not early enough. We met Mr. Hoogsteen coming up the road. His mournful yellow mustache stuck out over the collar of a tattered bearskin coat that reached to his heels, and he had so many clothes on underneath the coat that he waddled when he walked.

He said, "Good morning. You go get the ice from the river out already, huh?"

Father said reluctantly, "Well, I don't know. I was thinkin' about it. Nothin' better to do today."

"All right," said Mr. Hoogsteen. "I come help."

"Why, Bub and me——" father began. Mr. Hoogsteen's yellow mustache twitched slightly. "We'll be glad to have your company," father ended lamely. He nudged me to get off the spring seat to make room for the man.

At the bridge, father drove down the bank onto the ice, to a deep pool a little way downstream, and he went to work cutting a hole in the ice. It was almost three feet thick, so making this first cut was quite a little chore. Mr. Hoogsteen offered to help, but father wouldn't let him. There really wasn't much for Mr. Hoogsteen to do. By and by, when father finished the cut and started sawing, he helped me get out the tongs and tackle and hitch Sam to it, and set up the skids to the box on the sled.

We began snaking blocks out of the creek and up into the sled. Father handled the tongs, and I drove Sam, and Mr. Hoogsteen took up a peavey father had brought and helped steer the cakes onto the skids. The fur coat and all those clothes made him clumsy, but he would not put aside any of them.

Father cut good big blocks, and the work went fast; by mid-afternoon we had two loads hauled and a third nearly loaded, and had made an open hole ten feet square, maybe larger. The water was greenish black, with a scum of ice chips twisting in the slow eddies. The hole was scary to look at—a black, wide-open mouth in the snowy face of the stream.

We had the last block half out of the pool when the line fouled on a skid. Mr. Hoogsteen moved to free it, and the block of ice swerved toward him as the skid tilted. He jumped back and tangled his feet in the peavey, and plunged head first into the open water.

He made an enormous splash. Father yelled and I yelled, and Sam jumped and the line came free, jerking the tongs loose from the ice block, which followed Mr. Hoogsteen into the hole. I forgot Sam and ran to where father was bending over the edge of the pool, watching for Mr. Hoogsteen to come up. The current was sluggish, but he had gone in from the upstream side. If the plunge had taken him under the ice, there was nothing we could do for him.

We glimpsed a wavering movement deep in the water, and father looked around for the peavey, but Mr. Hoogsteen had taken it into the creek with him and it was out of reach, bobbing in the water. Father grabbed me and thrust me away from the hole.

Survivor or victim? Quickness of movement and thought on the part of the rescuers determines the outcome.

"The tongs!" he yelled. "Get that rig over here!"

Sam had wandered off a few yards and was standing watching us. By the time I had him backed around, Mr. Hoogsteen had come to the surface. He had managed to grab hold of the peavey—which, of course, was too light to be any use to him—with one hand and he was beating the water with the other, and he was gasping and choking and trying to holler and making big wooshing noises. He was too busy to take hold of the ax handle father was holding out to him, and too frightened even to see it.

Father leaned out over the pool as far as he dared, and put the ax handle against Mr. Hoogsteen and pushed hard. Mr. Hoogsteen went under the water, but the shove started him floating toward the lower side of the hole. Father picked up the tongs and ran around to meet him. When he came within reach, father snagged the back of his fur coat, and I started up Sam. Father gave a heave on his coat collar, and Mr. Hoogsteen came skittering out onto the ice. He lay there on his back, waggling his hands and feet feebly and turning his head from side to side, until we stood him up and started peeling wet clothes off him.

You would never believe how many clothes the man had on under that fur coat, all of them soaking wet and starting to freeze the moment the air hit them. Mr. Hoogsteen was too exhausted to help us; he toppled over, in whichever direction he happened to be pointed, whenever we let go of him. We got him stripped at last, and father took off his own shirt and rubbed him with it while I hitched the team to the sled. Father put his jacket and sheepskin coat on Mr. Hoogsteen and bundled the lap robe around him, and lifted him bodily into the seat. When I started to get in the sled, Father stopped me.

"You cut some of those fir trees," he said, "and build a fence around that hole, before some other damned fool falls in it."

He swung the team to break out the runners and started them up toward the road. It was an inspiring sight to see them racing away in a welter of flying ice with father in his red flannel undershirt standing up in the sled cracking their rumps with the line ends. They turned up the creek

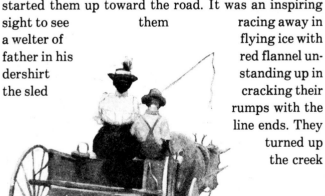

bank onto the road, and as the sled tilted, the load of ice blocks shot out of the rear end and came slithering down on the frozen surface of the stream. No one had thought to put in the tail gate.

Mr. Hoogsteen's gratitude for this rescue had practically no limit, and his expression of it by word and deed grew increasingly oppressive. He was as ruthless and obstinate as a child in his determination to show his appreciation. Only by downright brutality could father have put him off—and of this he was incapable.

The worst of it was that Mr. Hoogsteen told others the story, and father's rescue became famous over the countryside. So father refused to go outside his own fences. He would not go uptown for mail and supplies on a Saturday. So mother had to go, and could no longer do her baking on that day, which upset her schedule and her disposition.

The climax came on a day in early spring, a Sunday, when mother had gone to a sewing bee at Mrs. Cook's, who was expecting. Father and I were in the granary, sacking oats for seed, when Al Daveneck, the butcher from uptown, drove into the yard.

He said, "Howdy, Plimpton. Say, Hoogsteen ain't up here, is he?"

The question made father bristle. "No!" he snapped.

"All right," Daveneck said. "I just thought he might be. He ain't at home, and I understand he's up here a good deal, helpin', since you saved his hide."

He went on talking for a minute, but father's answers were so short that he didn't stay long. When he had gone, father went back in the granary.

"You hear that?" he asked me. "Now folks are thinkin' I make the little walrus work for me, takin' advantage of him! I got to do something—I got to!"

He sat there with his chin on his fists, staring past me out the door and groaning once in a while. Pretty soon I saw Mr. Hoogsteen going down the road toward his place. I mentioned it to father.

"He's not comin' in here, is he?"

I peeked through a crack. "No, he's went on by."

We better get on with the sackin'....Go get me a drink of water first, will you?"

I took a step toward the door, and father said, "Wait!" so sharply that I jumped. He was staring at our well, on the other side of the yard, as if he'd never seen it before.

It was a good well, dug, not drilled, and lined with fire-killed spruce poles. It was about thirty feet deep, and had twelve feet of water in it. Father walked over

and stood looking down into it while I pulled up a bucket of water. After we drank, he went down past the house to the road, and I followed. Far down the road, near the Moose Creek bridge, we could see Daveneck's rig going back toward town. The sound of ax blows came from the direction of Hoogsteen's house.

Father said, "Sounds as if Mr. Hoogsteen was at home. Choppin' wood, I guess."

"Sounds that way all right."

He turned and looked back toward our yard. "Bub," he said, "suppose you run along over to Mr. Hoogsteen's place and ask him if he'd step over here for a minute, give me a hand."

I stared at him, not believing my ears. "But—but why? What for?"

"Never you mind what for. You do as I tell you. Get along now—and don't waste time on the way."

I trudged away, mystified and resentful. Father's voice followed me: "What's the matter, you tied to somethin'? Come on; get those feet untracked!" His voice seemed to hold a note of excitement. When I looked back, he was hurrying toward the yard.

Mr. Hoogsteen was splitting wood in back of his cabin. I gave him father's message.

"Now already?" he asked.

"I guess so, yes, if it's handy."

He sighed, and struck his ax into the block and turned toward the road without a word.

When we came into our yard, father was not in sight. I looked in the granary, and called, and called again more loudly. I thought I could hear his voice answer me; it sounded hollow and muffled, and came from nowhere. And then I noticed that the cover had been taken off the well, and the rope was gone from the pulley. I screeched, "Mr. Hoogsteen!" and ran to the curbing and peered into the gloomy pit.

Father was in there. He was up to his neck in water. When he saw us he began to thrash around and yell. "Help! Help! I'm drowning! Get me out of here!"

There were crosspieces nailed to the casing to form a ladder, but I saw that those nearest the water had been broken off; the lowest was out of father's reach. I was dancing with fear and excitement, and so was Mr. Hoogsteen.

"We get you out, Mr. Plimpton!" he shouted. "Don't you worry, we get you out once!"

Father sank down in the water and made a noise like "Glub-glub-glub!"

I shrieked and Mr. Hoogsteen roared with alarm: "Stay up yet, Mr. Plimpton! I come help you quick now like everything!"

He flung off his coat and started to climb over the well curbing. Father put his head up out of the water. "A rope!" he called clearly. "Bub! Get that rope out of the granary! . . .Don't come down here, Hoogsteen!"

I brought the rope, and we reeved it through the block at the well head and knotted the end and pulled it on through. Father caught hold, and we took a turn under a brace and pulled together, hoisting him up until he could reach the ladder.

He climbed over the curbing, his teeth chattering and his lips blue with cold. He had the end of the well rope in his hand; he caught it quickly around the brace and reached for Mr. Hoogsteen.

"Neighbor," he said earnestly, "you saved my life

for certain
that time. I can't begin to thank you. If you
hadn't come along just when you did and pulled me out
of there, I might 'a' drowned!"

Mr. Hoogsteen beamed, and his mustache bristled
happily. "Yes, oh, yes," he said. "That's all right.
Sure! You save my life, I save your life. So?"

"That's it!" father said. "You got it just right! So
now we're even, hey? Fifty-fifty!"

The mustache drooped. "But wait yet a minute,"
Mr. Hoogsteen said. "Two times you have saved
me—with the disk once, with the ice once." He held up
two fingers. "And I—I have but once yet for you."

Father shivered violently. "You got to look at it this
way, Hoogsteen," he said. "A man ain't got but one
life, has he? Well then, it stands to reason—no matter
how many times you save it, it's still only one life. You
understand?"

Mr. Hoogsteen didn't look as if he understood, any
better than I did. He puzzled over it a while, and apparently decided to take father's word for it.

"So," he said, "you mean we got it even now?"

"Absolutely," said father. "Even-Stephen."

"All right," said Mr. Hoogsteen. "Shake hands."

They shook hands solemnly. Then Mr. Hoogsteen
drew a deep breath and stepped back, squaring his
puny shoulders. The mustache stood straight out, and
his eyes were fiery.

"And now," he said, "now, by golly, Mr. Plimpton, I
tell you something! You know what for I come to this
country? I come for get away from too many peoples
all the time already—too many neighbors, too many
relations, all the time too many everybodies all over
me! So what happens? So right away, by golly, you
start doing by me favors! Never can anything happen

but you go
to be there for
upgefixen! By the dog the
porcupine, by me the disk, by me
the river! All the time is something already!"

He was shouting and waving his fists angrily.
Father stood in slack-jawed astonishment, staring at
the little man.

"Mr. Plimpton, I tell you, when I think about all the
thankfulness I got to had to make for you, I could—I
could just—oh, by golly——"

Something in his eyes caused father to start back,
but too late. An irresistible impulse lifted Mr. Hoogsteen's right foot and launched it at father's shin. With
a wild yell of triumph, Mr. Hoogsteen turned and
streaked for home.

The blow was nothing, for Mr. Hoogsteen wore thick
rubber overshoes outside a felt boot. Father sat heavily upon the well curb, staring after the retreating
figure.

"Well, I'll be eternally——If that don't beat the
Dutch!" he said. "Why, the little rooster! Who'd ever
'a' thought the little rooster was that full o' hell and independence? . . . You know, I never really thought
before I'd like the man!"

There was a claw hammer sticking out of father's hip
pocket. Down in the well, just below the water level, a
perfectly sound crosspiece was still nailed to the casing, and another underneath it. The missing pieces left
no more than a three-foot gap in the ladder.

I looked at these things, and at father, and when he
saw my face he grinned a slow, sheepish grin.

"Think you got somethin' all figured out, don't
you?" he said. "Well, if you're smart as you think you
are, you'll keep it to yourself. Understand?"

His glance wandered to his sodden garments, and he
frowned. "Bub," he said, "whatever do you suppose
I'm goin' to tell your mother about this?" (1939)

The *Tourist* and the *Tenderfoot*

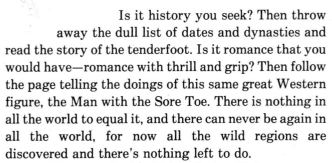

The Tenderfoot

An Essay by
Emerson Hough

Is it history you seek? Then throw away the dull list of dates and dynasties and read the story of the tenderfoot. Is it romance that you would have—romance with thrill and grip? Then follow the page telling the doings of this same great Western figure, the Man with the Sore Toe. There is nothing in all the world to equal it, and there can never be again in all the world, for now all the wild regions are discovered and there's nothing left to do.

Everything in the world is relative. Today our tenderfeet travel West in palace cars, and build cottages in Los Angeles, where they settle down and call themselves "Western" in spite of their entire Easterness. Once they traveled in stagecoaches, or plodded alongside of ox teams, or hoofed it straight. The supply of tenderfeet under one name or the other is something perennial. There are as many now east of the Mississippi as ever went West in any era of the world. From now on until the end of time there will ever appear, drifting across the page of record, that most laughable and most lovable of all Western characters, the Tenderfoot—rapt, entranced, open-mouthed and sore-toed.

No one knows the inglorious Webster who first invented this generic title, but it could not be improved upon in a score of dictionaries, and could not be defined in a page of explanation. It covers a volume of endeavor, folly, pluck, romance, hope, failure, despair, cheerfulness, life and death. The picture is perfectly obvious: some horny-footed son of toil sat grinning at his shack door, and said, "Evenin', stranger!" to the man who limped up and stood on the side of his foot as he talked; "feet a little tender, eh?"

Thus, no doubt, it began. Always there was the supercilious attitude of the man already there. Suppose Cabeza de Vaca had met Coronado toiling along in his iron hat and steel trousers in the scorching sun of the Panhandle desert; what would he have said? Blithely he would have inquired, "You blooming tenderfoot, what are you doing out West?" And Coronado, away, back in 1513, would have smiled at Cabeza de Vaca; and so on. But always the tenderfoot pressed on, wide-eyed, hopeful, following the sun.

The tenderfoot—especially the tenderfoot who has discovered the West with the deliberate intention of informing the East about it—is careful to call attention to his "chaps"; and it may be some time before he learns that cow-punchers call them leggins. He may for a time mention his "lariat," because he has read about that somewhere; but it will not be long before he calls it "rope," as everyone else does. In the Middle West he will never hear of a "lasso." That is Californian, where it sometimes is also called "lass." It will be longer before the tenderfoot learns the technical names of different makes of saddles, and knows a "Menier tree" from an apple orchard; or can explain the difference between a centre fire and a Texas saddle, or discourse learnedly as to the merits of rope-tied or rope-wrapped—à la Texas or à la California—or is able to talk wisely of the merits of the Mexican stirrup and tapadera as against the round-bottom stirrup. He hears the last-named stirrup is safer for riding "outlaws," and after a while learns that an "outlaw" is a horse and not a bad man. It is still later, perhaps, before he learns to take out a scar-backed and saddle-worn mount from the corral instead of the sleek, smooth-backed, carefree looking animal, which is so much more attractive in appearance. That is where he learns that the wicked are smug—and discovers what an "outlaw" really is.

When the tenderfoot is camping out he builds a big fire. The man whom he calls a "native" does not. A large fire is wasteful, wearisome, uncomfortable and dangerous, and one can neither cook nor be warmed at it. On the plains he does not know what the native means who asks him to gather up some "chips" and make a fire, until he remembers reading of the bois des vaches—what the men of the lower ranges still call "boonyeegers," the only fuel of the plains for the men antedating crops or transportation. The tenderfoot always rolls up in his bed—when he is so far along in Western education as to venture to sleep without a tent—and lies down with his head to the wind. This is wrong, as is almost everything else he does. The old-timer, of course, sleeps with his feet to the wind, so that the bed covering will not be blown loose and that the air may not get in so freely around his neck at the open part of the blankets. In the gray of morning the coyotes call, and the tenderfoot has a sensation. At breakfast—when he invariably cooks the bacon too much—he nonchalantly asks the old-timer if he "heard the wolves howl this morning." "No,"˝answers the other, "but it seems to me that I did hear a coyote yipping a little while ago." The tenderfoot calls that *koi*-ote; the Westerner always calls it *ki*-ote, unless he is a native of the far Southwest, where the Mexicans call it ki-*o*-te.

For a long time the tenderfoot is guilty of the unpardonable solecism of speaking of "cattle" instead of "cows"; forgetting that on the range proper all horned animals are "cows," no matter what

their sex. He assumes the term "bronco" to mean all horses, which is wrong—for there are many sorts of horses recognized in the West.

The tenderfoot will for a long time climb into his saddle by a hand-grasp on the cantle; which means, of course, that he must take his hand off the cantle as he swings his right leg over and into place. After he has done that a few times with one of those things which he calls a "broncho," and which he may perhaps recognize as an "outlaw," he will understand why a cowpuncher never touches a cantle, but makes a close connection with the pommel—which he himself calls "horn"—perhaps turning the stirrup square out, or, perhaps, even facing to the rear, with the stirrup twisted around to the front, before he makes his first spring for the saddle seat. This position, of course, pulls a man up and into the saddle if the horse rears or plunges. The tenderfoot will learn this in time, and will learn to "circle"

Sore bottom, injured pride, tenderfoot.

his horse with his left hand, pulling the head sharply in if he finds his horse "mean"—which is another Western word whose significance he has learned anew.

There are a thousand and one things which the tenderfoot does or does not do which betray him to be a tenderfoot after he has long thought himself something otherwise; but gradually he is winning his degree—that most valuable of all a man's degrees in education—in the school of the plains and of the mountains. When he rides his first pitching horse, and kills his first antelope, and gets lost and sleeps out alone for a couple of nights, he writes home and tells his sister all about it—or some other man's sister. When he does all these things by second nature, without thinking about it, then he is no longer tenderfoot but Western man. Perhaps by this time he has used up the money sent from home, and has learned how to make a living for himself in the country that he now thinks of as home. He is, then, in a position to be Cabeza de Vaca, and to smile patronizingly at Coronado from Harvard as he limps along, Westward bound. (1906)

If the stance feels as natural as it looks, then chances are he is no longer tenderfoot, but Western man.

The Simple Tourist

Observations by Irvin S. Cobb

When I go forth with intent to waylay the simple tourist I am preying on my own kind. It takes more than two or three trips West to cure an Easterner of the habit of being a tourist and to make a regular human being of him. Merely because he has learned the difference between spinach and mesquite does not qualify him to pass judgment on the rest of his breed. Myself, I still suffer from a tenderness of the feet.

This has been a great year—this year of 1915—for eastern America and western America too; the best year, in some regards, these two great major divisions of our common country ever had. Because of the war that has been proceeding on the other hemisphere, those who ordinarily would have gone off to Europe, Asia and Africa have had to stick round. There was nothing else for them to do; so they did it. The excessively wealthy classes have traveled about over their own land and viewed the peasantry through their lorgnettes. The moderately well-to-do, who other years would have been saving up to give their money to the custodians of art galleries in foreign parts, have followed suit, doing the same thing, without the lorgnette effect. The celebration of Old Home Continent has been a success in every particular. To date the management has yet to hear a single complaint.

The transcontinental trunk lines never carried so many passengers back and forth within the same space of time. The resort hotels of the West have had the most prosperous season they have ever had. Millions of dollars have been spent at home that otherwise would have gone into the bottomless pockets of European shopkeepers. From a sentimental standpoint, the value of the intercourse has been even greater than its material value has been.

All joking aside, the East has become better acquainted with the West—the West, being more progressive, already knew the East pretty well. And a great many thousands of persons have got acquainted with their own country; with its natural wonders—and with its man-made wonders, too, which in their way are just as wonderful. With their own eyes they have seen that there is still a part of North America which does not have "no trespass" signs on it; which is not even fenced in. They have taken occasion to observe that between the Mississippi River and the Pacific Slope is a fairly considerable acreage.

They feel themselves to be Balboas and Ponce de Leons. They have discovered the other side of North America. Little Jack Horner has come out of his corner and (having ventured forth) is most gratified with the results.

To be sure, the West, geographically considered, is not exactly brand-new. As a scenic production the West has been going on for some time now. Our tourist brother might have seen it last year, or last century, if he had been round then.

All this long while it has been waiting for him to come along and give it his approval—the Painted Desert, where the Almighty took the tail of a rainbow for a paintbrush and dipped it in the sunset and limned an illimitable canvas in colors which never glowed on the palette of any human artist; that other and greater desert, where, since time began, the cracked and naked pelt of the earth had been pegged out, drying in the suns of all eternity; and, adventurous man, invading a blistered desolation that might have daunted the soul of a salamander, has, with a spade in his hand and a vision before his eyes, wrought it into the fairest and the greenest and the richest of garden spots on this hemisphere; the mountains—not one mighty range, but a dozen, and each of them seeming mightier than the last; the big trees; Yellowstone Park and Glacier National Park, filled with the unfinished jobs of creation; Yosemite and Lake Tahoe; Monterey Bay and the Golden Gate; the Indian country of the Northwest, where Sitting Bull refused to be seated and the restless Spotted Tail so frequently changed his spots; the Indian country of the Southwest, where the cliff dwellers founded a civilization as old as Egypt's, and where today the Navajo tends his flocks—or would do so if he were not so busy selling blankets; the Lava Beds and the Staked Plains; the Black Hills and the Bad Lands; and—greater than any of these and greatest of all the cataclysmic convulsions of Nature—the Grand Canyon, which no one ever yet has properly described, though nearly everyone has had a try at it.

I violate no confidence in stating that these things have been continuing without interruption for a considerable period; but a good many of us are just finding out about them. . . .

On the morning of my arrival at the Grand Canyon there arrived also a lady from somewhere back East, traveling alone, who undertook to walk down the canyon and back up again the same day. One like her comes about once in so often. This lady had a determined manner and one of those figures that seem to overlap. Just by looking at her you knew that the menfolks of her family, on both sides for several generations back, had been what are known as steady providers. Also, instinctively as it were, you gathered that she was prominent in reform movements, uplift waves and clubs generally; she had that air about her.

They argued with her—the guides and others—when,

after taking a look into that mighty void, she announced her intention of making the journey up and down Bright Angel Trail afoot; they tried to dissuade her. But, no; this lady was not to be deterred. She stated that she would just stroll down during the forenoon and eat her lunch, and pluck a few wild flowers at Indian Gardens, which she could see very plainly from where she stood, and then in the afternoon she would stroll back.

We started, too, but on muleback and in another direction. I was riding a mule with a neat pompadour on her high, intellectual forehead and a carefully shingled tail, named Chiquita, meaning, in Spanish, Little One; which was a joke, because this mule was not little. The time before when I visited the canyon I rode a mule called Martha. I rode her for three days; and never after that, they told me, was she the mule she had been. She seemed to pine away and grow morose; and every time another fat man appeared in riding togs and the guide approached her, bearing a saddle, she just laid down on her side and uttered low moans. I judge she suffered from melancholia or something of that general nature; so now I had Chiquita for a mount.

We headed down the Hermit Trail. When we came to the first signpost on the journey Chiquita stopped dead still and read what it said. And when she read that we had gone only 800 feet below the level of the rim and had yet nearly 4,000 feet to go, measuring straight downward—or nine miles as the trail ran—realization seemed to come to her, and she turned and put her head on my shoulder and sobbed out the sorrow of her heart. I joined with her; for I remember that it had been more than a year since I had ridden in a saddle, and this was a very hard saddle. And I am by nature most tender,

When tourists and natives get together,
it can be hard to tell who's doing the sightseeing.

if you get my meaning. There, on the narrow ledge overhanging the abysmal depths, our tears mingled.

Shortly afterward my attention was distracted. The scientist with the whiskers sat down in his white-duck riding pants on a cactus bed. But, before that, the young lady from Waukesha pulled her mule out of line and hurried him forward from the middle of the

cavalcade to the head of it, so she might ask Shorty, who was our chief guide for that day, some questions that had been accumulating and backing up in her during the earlier stages of the expedition. She had been repeatedly assured in various quarters that she was perfectly safe, and that the trail was perfectly safe, and that everything was perfectly safe; but still she craved confirmation from an expert and experienced source.

"Now tell me honestly," she demanded, "isn't

East is east, west is west and never the twain shall meet—until the bold New Englander ventures into cowboy country.

W.H.D. Koerner (1878-1938)

there any danger at all connected with this ride?''

"Ma'am," said Shorty seriously, "since you put it up to me that way, I ain't going to deceive you. If Slim's wife is running things down to the foot of the trail everything is all right, and you needn't worry; but if she should 'a' happened to leave camp and Slim should be doing the cooking, and we should have to eat his cooking tonight for supper, this shore is what you might call a dangerous and perilous journey."

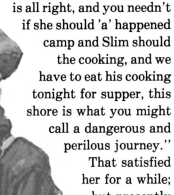

That satisfied her for a while; but presently she saw one of those little monuments of piled-up boulders the canyon prospectors leave behind them to mark the locations of their mining claims, and she wanted to know what that was. The guides are always set and loaded for that question; they know that sometime during the trip, sooner or later, it is coming, and they are primed for it.

"That, ma'am," said Shorty in an Alas-poor-Yorick-I-knew-him-well tone, "is the grave of a poor old trail guide."

Shorty was waiting for someone of the party to ask what caused the death of the late lamented, so that he might reply, according to the ancient ritual, that he was talked to death by tourists. . . .

Shorty's fears were unfounded. Slim was not doing the cooking when we reached the camp at the foot of Hermit Trail. Mrs. Slim was in charge, and very soon we discovered that she knew a good deal about bringing out the best points of biscuit dough and frying-size beefsteaks and flapjack batter. I noticed a lot of modern improvements that had taken place in the camp since my last call.

There were even some patent fire extinguishers, shaped like Roman candles, hanging upon the walls of the mess hall. Somehow they looked a little bit out of place away down there in the bowels of the earth; but I guess they were regarded as necessary, for, though the canyon may never catch fire, being constructed almost exclusively of strictly inflammable materials, the camp might. And, seeing that the nearest regular paid fire department is about 90 miles away across the desert, with a gash a mile deep and 13 miles wide in between, you might safely figure that if a fire broke out, say, on a Thursday, and the alarm were sent in promptly, it would be along about Sunday afternoon before the engines showed up; and by that time the fire would probably have grown tired of waiting for them and quit of its own accord.

Late the next day, as we were nearing the top of the canyon, we met a lone guide coming down with a burro pack train, and he stopped long enough to tell us the finish of the story concerning the iron-jawed lady who had insisted the morning before on walking down Bright Angel Trail.

Shortly before dusk of the same day someone passing through the Indian Gardens had heard her pants for help, and he telephoned up; and a rescue expedition was organized and sent down for the lady. She made the return trip on a mule or a couple of mules—I forget which—with a guide walking at each side, holding her hands; and when she reached the rim she went to pieces like a glass snake. . . .

Yes, I shall be trailing the Simple Tourist in Arizona late this fall. If I should not meet him there, I shall seek him at the expositions; and if I fail to discover a typical specimen either in San Francisco or in San Diego, I shall look in the mirror—and there I know I shall find one. (1915)

Now taken for granted, the road that beckons us to America's scenic wonders was a major breakthrough in its time.

The Keys to the Park

An Editorial by **Will Payne**

They would not let President Taft see the Grand Canyon of the Colorado from the bottom—although the Grand Canyon, we should say, is the greatest scenic possession of the United States; even the greatest scenic possession of the world—because the only descent is by horseback over a steep and tortuous trail, and in the opinion of the responsible judges he is not suitably constructed for that method of locomotion.

For all the national parks roadmaking is a chief concern. Mere conservation is only the beginning of an intelligent park policy. To make the parks as accessible as possible without defacing them is quite as important as merely preserving them. Having a beautiful park that nobody, or hardly anybody, can see is as wasteful as burying a beautiful painting out of sight. The use of the thing is lost.

Good roads are the first factor in accessibility. They are the key that opens the parks to you. (1915)

How Do You Like the Climate?

An Essay by Irvin S. Cobb

Once upon a time a stranger went to Southern California; and when he was asked the customary question—to wit: "How do you like the climate?"—he said: "No, I don't like it!" So they destroyed him on the spot. I have forgotten now whether they just hanged him on the nearest tree or burned him at the stake; but they destroyed him utterly and hid his bones in an unmarked grave.

History, that lying jade, records that when Balboa first saw the Pacific he plunged breast-deep into the waves, drew his sword and waved it on high, probably using for that purpose the Australian crawl stroke; and then, in that generous and carefree way of the early discoverers, claimed the ocean and all points west in the name of his Catholic Majesty, Carlos the Cutup, or Pedro the Impossible, or whoever happened to be the king of Spain at that moment. Personal investigation convinces me that the current version of the above incident was wrong.

What Balboa did first was to state that he liked the climate better than any climate he'd ever met; was perfectly crazy about it, in fact, and intended to sell out back East and move West just as soon as he could get word home to his folks; after which, still following

the custom of the country, he bought a couple of Navajo blankets and some moccasins with blue beadwork on the toes, mailed a few souvenir postcards to close friends, and had his photograph taken standing in the midst of the tropical verdure, with a freshly picked orange in his hand. And if he waved his sword at all it was with the idea of forcing the real estate agents to stand back and give him air. I am sure that these are the correct details, because that is what every round-tripper does upon arriving in Southern California; and, though Balboa finished his explorations at a point some distance below the California line, nevertheless, and to the contrary notwithstanding, he was still in the climate belt. Life out there in that fair land is predicated on climate; out there climate is capitalized, organized and systematized. Every native is a climate booster; so is every newcomer as soon as he has stuck round long enough to get the climate habit, which is in from one to three days. They talk climate; they think climate; they breathe it by day; they snore it by night; and in between times they live on it. And it is good living, too—especially for the real estate people and the hotel keepers.

Southern Californians brag of their climate just as New York brags of its wickedness and its skyscrapers, and as Richmond brags of its cooking and its war memories. I don't blame them either; the California climate is worth all the brags it gets. Back East in the wintertime we have weather; out in Southern California they never have weather—nothing but climate. For hours on hours a native will stand outdoors, with his hat off and his head thrown back, inhaling climate until you can hear his nostrils smack. And after you've been on the spot a day or two you're doing the same thing yourself, for, in addition to being salubrious, the California climate is catching.

Going northward or southward in California, your road lies between mountains. To the eastward, shutting out the deserts from this domain of everlasting summer, are the Sierras—great saw-edged old he-mountains, masculine as bulls or bucks, all rugged and wrinkled, bearded with firs and pines upon their jowls,

California: a mixture of the finest nature has to offer in scenery and climate, with a little Mexican flavoring added.

A horse needs little guidance along California's scenic route, a path so wide, long and lush, it's hard to stray from.

but baldheaded and hoar with age at top like the prophets of old. But the mountains of the Coast Range, to the westward, are full-bosomed and maternal, mothering the valleys up to them; and their round-uddered, fecund slopes are covered with softest green. Only when you come closer to them you see that the garments on their breasts are not really silky-smooth as they looked at a distance, but shirred and gored, gathered and smocked. I suppose even a lady mountain never gets too old or too settled to follow the fashions!

Now you pass an orchard big enough to make a hundred of your average Eastern orchards; and if it be of apples or plums or cherries, and the time be springtime, it is all one vast white bridal bouquet; but if it be of almonds or peaches the whole land, maybe for miles on end, will blaze with a pink flame that is the pinkest pink in the world—pinker than the heart of a ripe watermelon.

Here is a meadowland of purest, deepest green; and flung across it, like a streak of sunshine playing hooky

from heaven, is a slash of wild yellow poppies. There, upon a hillside, stands a clump of gnarly, dwarfed olives, making you think of Bible times and the Old Testament. Or else it is a great ranch, where cattle by thousands feed upon the slopes. Or a crested ridge, upon which the gum trees stand up in long aisles, sorrowful and majestic as the funereal groves of the ancient Greeks—that is, provided it was the ancient Greeks who had the funereal groves.

Or, best of all and most striking in its contrasts, you will see a cut-plush hill, with a nap on it like a family album; and right on the top of it an old, crumbly graystone mission, its cross gleaming against the skyline; and, down below, a modern town, with red roofs and hipped windows, its houses buried to their eaves in palms and giant rose bushes, and huge climbing geraniums, and all manner of green tropical growths that are nature's own Christmas trees, with the red-and-yellow dingle-dangles growing upon them. Or perhaps it is a gorge choked with the enormous redwoods, each individual tree with a trunk like the Washington Monument. And, if you are only as lucky as we were, up overhead, across the blue sky, will be drifting a hundred fleecy clouds, one behind the other, like woolly white sheep.

Everywhere the colors are splashed on with a barbaric, almost a theatrical, touch. It's a regular backdrop of a country; its scenery looks as though it belonged on a stage—as though it should be painted on a curtain. You almost expect to see a chorus of comic opera brigands or a bevy of stage milkmaids come trooping out of the wings any minute. Who was the libelous wretch who said that the flowers of Southern California had no perfume and the birds there had no song? Where we passed through tangled woods the odors distilled from the wild flowers by the sun's warmth were almost suffocating in their sweetness; and in a flowered bush on the lawn at Coronado I came upon a mocking bird singing in a way to make his brother minstrel of Mobile or Savannah feel like applying for admission to a school of expression and learning the singing business all over again.

At the end of the valley—top end or bottom end as the case may be—you come to a chain of lesser moun-

tains, dropped down across your path like a trailing wing of the Indians' fabled thunderbird, vainly trying to shut you out from the next valley. You climb the divide and run through the pass, with a brawling river upon one side and tall cliffs upon the other; and then all of a sudden the hills magically part and you are within sight—almost within touch—of the ocean; for in this favored land the mountains come right down to the sea and the sea comes right up to the mountains. It may be upon a tiny bay that you have emerged, with the meadows sloping straight to tidemark, and out beyond the wild fowl feeding by the kelp beds.

Or perhaps you have come out upon a ragged, rugged headland, crowned belike with a single wind-twisted tree, grotesquely suggesting a frizzled chicken; and down below, straight and sheer, are the rocks rising out of the water like the jaws of a mangle. Down there in that ginlike reef Neptune is forever washing out his shirt in a smother of foamy lather. And he has spilled his bluing pot, too—else how could the sea be so blue? On the outermost rocks the sea lions have stretched themselves, looking like so many overgrown slugs; and they lie there and sun themselves and bellow—or, at least, I am told they do so on occasion. There was unfortunately no bellowing going on the day I was there.

The unearthly beauty of the whole thing overpowers you. The poet that lives in nearly every human soul rouses within you, and you feel like withdrawing to yon dense grove or yon peaked promontory to commune with Nature. But be advised in season. Restrain yourself! Carefully refrain! Do not do so! Because out from under a rock somewhere will crawl a real estate agent to ask you how you like the climate and then to take a dollar down from you as first payment on a fruit ranch, or a suburban lot, or a seaside villa—or something. (1913)

Balanced precariously on the mountainside, man and beast struggle to meet the rigorous demands of a cattle drive.

Big Dude Drive

A Yarn by Anne Chamberlin

The Pioneers, where now are they?
Those sturdy men so brave and true
Who met the Indians in the fray
And gave the savage foe his due;
Who faced the storms of wind and rain
When whacking bulls across the plains?

"To the Pioneers of Montana," by W.L. Davies,
published by The Pioneer Society of Sweet Grass
County, Montana.

I can tell you exactly where they are, Mr. Davies.
They're out there on the plains right now, with their
bones aching, blisters on their knees, hair stiffening in
the hot wind, throats parched, a cold Spam sandwich in
their saddlebags and a song in their hearts. Only they're
not called pioneers any more, they're called *dudes.* And
they *pay* to whack those bulls across the plains.

Back at the dude ranch, with the long day's hardships behind him, the same happy pioneer can splash
the dust off his face in a tin washbasin, with a tin pitch-
erful of water he has fetched for himself from the
community shower house up on the hill. He can dress
by the light of a bare bulb dangling from a beam in his
log cabin, gulp a Martini from a paper cup, if he
remembered to stop for ice on the way up from the corral, and dash obediently to the dining hall when the
dinner bell tolls.

With no extra charge for saddlesores, bruises and
mosquito bites, sharing the joys and perils of ranch life
only costs a few hundred a week. At one ranch you can
even help drive cows into summer pastures in the

Crazy Mountains. But working *that* hard costs extra.

When the first dude (a Western term for an Eastern
guest) offered back in 1879 to *pay* Howard Eaton and
his brothers to hang around their cattle ranch in the
Bad Lands of South Dakota—and even lend a hand
with the chores—the Eatons couldn't believe it.

They "felt a little awkward at first, taking the
money," a recent account admits, "but the guest convinced them it was a smart business proposition
beneficial to both sides." And thus was born one of the
most heart-warming commercial relationships in the
whole American Way of Life.

It may take the dudes a whole summer to wrestle the
calves that the pros could rope and brand in a day. (Some
ranchers confine the guests to such work as riding,
fishing, hunting, hiking, picnicking and camping, prefer-
ring to cultivate livestock *or* dudes, but not both.) But
the money the dudes pay to complicate things can keep a
small cattle rancher from going broke. And the dudes
come back, as one rancher says, "Kicked, bruised—and
thinking they've had a good time."

With this kind of spirit loose among the volunteers,
it's naturally the *hired* help that's hard to come by.
The old-time wrangler, that lean-jawed, blue-eyed,
slim-hipped fellow in the faded jeans, who could strum
a guitar and remember the words to *Streets of Laredo*,
is succeeding the buffalo, the Indian and the bald eagle
as the Vanishing American. A friend of mine spotted
only one in a whole summer. He was leaning against
the doorway of a cafe, his Stetson jammed over his
eyes, as though he had been painted there by Frederic

Remington. . .and he was sipping a low-cal drink. The others have married the lady dudes of yesteryear and gone East. Or gone off to higher-paying jobs in the cities. Some would rather deal with cattle all year round than cope with two-legged guests for the short dude season.

A partial solution is the "W.D.," or working dude—a young man who works for his keep, mingles with the guests, but only gets to ride when there is a horse to spare. There is no trouble finding college girls to help around the cabins and wait on tables, but most of their application letters say they are dying to see the West and crazy about horses—with not much about what work they are prepared to do.

One rancher outlines a dismal summer with a seven-day week and no riding, and then hires the survivors who write back. But many cries for fry cooks, chore boys and dishwashers echo unanswered through the yucca at the height of the season.

Choosing one's ranch can be as touchy as selecting one's obstetrician—and no two are alike. The upholstered ver-

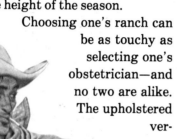

sions, complete with wall-to-wall rugs and heated pools, are called Resort Ranches. Others, which call themselves ranches, are referred to in the trade somewhat facetiously as "motels with horses."

But the classic genre has no TV, no air conditioning, no Muzak, a squeaky telephone on a party line, no Watusi, no Frug. On Saturday nights it's the Barnacle Bill and the Hokey Pokey to a recorded square-dance band. At one ranch there are also no radios, no newspapers, no drink machines, no potato chips—and no between-meal sales by the ice-cream truck. A Beatle-haired teen-ager who showed up at one ranch this summer was offered the choice of heading straight back to the barber in Cody or letting the rancher have after him with the sheep shears. Another, who asked for a sleeping pill, slept fine after he got told that "Lewis and Clark didn't have sleeping pills; if you're sleepy enough you'll sleep."

But keeping life simple seems to get more complicated every year. First it was inside plumbing and electricity. Now individual bathrooms in the cabins are threatening the community shower house, once the social center of the ranch. No one knows where progress will strike next.

Once in a while a new dude will gaze wildly about him at the hard-won homespun virtues of ranch life and flee into the night. A couple recently retreated from the X Bar A Ranch near McLeod, Montana, because they found no water skiing. There was a new swimming pool, all right, the dudes in residence poured concrete for it after they finished building the corral. No water skiing, however.

But the dudes who stay have left touching reminders all over the West that there is no more dedicated worker than the fellow who is paying for the privilege. Two surgeons staying at Turner's Triangle X Ranch in Moose, Wyoming, thought the place would look better with a formal gateway at the entrance. They chopped down three huge pines, hauled them out of the woods by mule, had their wives peel the bark off, hammered together a rustic arch of triumph that is a landmark of the area. At Siggins Triangle X Ranch a guest who came to hunt bears stayed to redo all the window frames. The morning I stopped by there for breakfast I found that the young ladies vacationing from a refined New England boarding school had already oiled all the saddles in the tack room, and were out in the kitchen helping with the

Talking one's way into the job is not impossible; handling what one has talked oneself into could prove to be.

dishes. Some of the grown-ups had cheerfully stayed up half the night making sandwiches and crating 40 dozen eggs for the departing pack trip. Guests who missed a wooden Killiloo bird which had once decorated a roof at Lazy K Bar Ranch in Big Timber, Montana, located it, rebuilt it, repainted it and reinstalled it where it belonged.

The Lazy K Bar Ranch, which is operated by the Paul Van Cleve family, offers one of the most stirring examples of the rancher-dude relationship. Not only are guests allowed to wrestle the calves at branding time, but if they pay extra, and sign up in advance, they can help Paul Van Cleve III and his daughter Barbara drive 200 cows and calves into summer pastures in the Crazy Mountains.

This last endeavor, which involves five nights in a sleeping bag and six days in the saddle, in rain, wind, hail, dust, oven heat and mountain chill, is usually so popular that several volunteers must be tactfully turned away. "We've had as many as thirty dudes help with the cattle," Mr. Van Cleve told me with Western candor. "And it was absolute chaos. It took two weeks to gather them all up." I think he was referring to the cows.

Although the Van Cleveses only added dudes to their stock after the slump in cattle prices in 1922, they represent a dynasty as formidable in Montana as the Kennedys in Massachusetts. Paul senior was the first Van Cleve to head West. He moved to Billings from Minneapolis in 1882, got to know the great Crow Indian chief, Plenty Coups, and killed rattlesnakes on the main street. He homesteaded

near Melville, a town whose population has exploded to 15, about eight miles from the present ranch. He built a 36-room house with a polo field and many garages for his own air-cooled Franklin automobile and those of his many Eastern guests, who came to try the fishing, buy his Thoroughbred horses and court his four daughters.

The original ranch house burned down, but the billiard table, said to be out of a Melville sporting house, and the upright piano, which has not been tuned since 1916, are in the main lodge of Lazy K Bar today.

After a day of dealing with a herd of stubborn Black Angus, a moment of playfulness was definitely in order.

The ranch is medium-sized by Western standards, which is to say that their nearest neighbor lives about eight miles away, and it takes a full day in a Jeep to visit the accessible parts of the property, which also includes three lakes and an 11,214-foot mountain, the highest peak of the Crazies.

The night before our cow-punching expedition started, Barbie Van Cleve gave us an indoctrination preview with colored slides, saying that, "When you get the cattle in, you'd be surprised how happy you'll feel." And she was absolutely right. There is hardly anything that can happen to me now that won't seem a little easier than persuading 200 howling Black Angus cows and their stubborn stiff-legged calves to quit munching the grass, stop sloshing in the "crick," and come out from under the thickets and start traveling uphill.

The Van Cleves easily convinced the *people* that the high pastures were greener, but not all the *cows* wanted to sign up. One strong-willed mother with a tottering week-old calf took every shunpike detour it was possible to take, and several that were not. Every single one of us dudes had a whack at trying to guide her, and all we had to show for it were bramble scratches and tired lungs.

"If an old cow goes up in the timber, just stop and cuss her a little," Spike advised us. "If you go after them, they'll head for the mountain and you'll never get them."

Spike had a loud noise he could make that the cows recognized as a voice of authority. Having been brought up on the coast of Maine, I can make no authoritative animal noise except to bark like a seal. And to do it right I have to flap my flippers together in front, which means dropping the reins, which would put even a *trained* seal at a disadvantage.

Reaching an understanding with one's horse, I should point out, is the clue to a dude's survival in the West, and not even a computerized personnel system could match the subtle skill that goes into matching a newcomer and his mount. He must be assigned a steed vigorous enough to satisfy his image of his horsemanship, but not so vigorous as to wipe him off on a cliff. "I can tell when they're under- or overestimating themselves—and I'm lucky," Spike Van Cleve says. The fellow who demanded the meanest horse on the ranch, and "wouldn't be put off by the next worst," was assigned one called Two Lair, which bucked him off 17 times and climbed a tree behind the laundry. Spike looked me in the eye, mentally calculated my beam as viewed from the rear, and assigned me a medium saddle, number 29, and a silvery gray mare named Sleet.

Sleet steered easily and had several forward speeds. One was called a jog, which only jarred the molars. The lope rattled the whole skeleton. She also had a full trot, which I tried to avoid, because even Spike used to say that "a full trot is a dirty gait." At night, when Sleet got rid of me, she would roll in the grass.

My first day at Lazy K Ranch I decided to get acquainted with Sleet on what was described as "a very short afternoon ride." We were gone three and a half hours, during which time we rode through the woods, across a stream, along a road, through a meadow, up the side of a mountain ("Lean forward and grab a hunk of mane"), across a stream, through forests, across a stream, through two gates, across a stream, partway up another mountain where we got off, tied our horses to trees and climbed the rest of the way on foot, being careful not to stick our hands in any crevices, because of the rattlesnakes. Then back down the mountain, up on the horses, and field, stream, woods, stream, road, stream, trail, stream until we finally caught sight of the corral.

We either forded 18 streams or forded the same stream 18 times. The only thing that saved me for the pack trip, colt branding, calf branding and cattle drive that lay ahead was that the next day was Sunday. And Sunday is the horses' day off.

Our dude team for the cattle drive was a taut little

band made up of Haywood Davis, a college student from North Carolina, and his younger brother Tom; Bill Phillips, 13, from Ridgefield, Connecticut; Mr. Walter Milliken, a chemical engineer on vacation from Du Pont's New York office, and Mrs. George Oliver, wife of a Pittsburgh banker who sensibly stayed back at the ranch with their children. Our leaders were Spike and Barbie and their neighbor Marian Whidden, who had pale blonde hair, rode a huge white horse and could make a noise that scared cows even more than Spike.

Barbie pitched the tents, remembered the toilet paper and bug spray, planned the meals, could make canned tuna taste like *quenelles de brochet* and played the guitar. Mr. Milliken washed the dishes, while Mrs. Oliver and I criticized the forks and dried. The young men dug a pit for garbage and fetched the water from the creek. Since Barbie also remembered to bring soap and towels, the ladies bathed upstream in the creek, where the horses drank, and the gents bathed around the bend where we cooled the beer. It was a lot more eventful way to get clean than back home in a bathtub. Mr. Milliken, rolling over to get the soap off, bruised his nose on a submerged boulder and lost his wash cloth in the fast current. For myself it is the first time I can remember looking up from brushing my teeth to find two deer staring at me.

Sleeping out there under the stars took a little getting used to. The first night, which we spent at a place called the Cow Camp, I put my sleeping bag on the back porch because Barbie said it had a beautiful view. It certainly did. I saw it clearly through unclosed eyes every minute of the night. My head was against a big bag of oats we'd brought for the horses' breakfast, and next morning when I asked Barbie if she thought it had been a mouse making that noise in my pillow, she said it probably was. There is a lot of that kind of sangfroid in the West.

The next night we shifted to a base camp in a meadow in Sweet Grass Canyon. This time my sleeping bag was inside a rubberized envelope about big enough for a police dog, which Barbie explained as a two-man Alpine tent left over from World War II. Small as it was, looking for my drugstore flashlight in the dark reminded me of the time Mark Twain logged

47 miles on his pedometer while crawling around his hotel room looking for his socks.

Robert McConaughy of R Lazy S Ranch in Moose, Wyoming, had told me that, "Next to no injuries, waking up and hearing the horse bells is the mark of a successful trip." Mrs. Oliver and I, who had our Alpine tents in what turned out to be the horses' all-night grazing ground, felt it was more like taking part in the Charge of the Light Brigade. We whiled away many a happy hour wondering whether a horse would (a) eat our tents, or (b) step on the quavering occupants.

My notes taken on those eventful days are coffee-stained, stuck together with pancake syrup and thoroughly mashed from a long journey in the back pocket of my blue brushed ladies' Levis from Ernst's Saddlery in Sheridan, Wyoming. But I can testify that the first day, after sharing a dawn breakfast of Wheaties, Wackies, scrambled eggs and pancakes with the haying crew at the home ranch, we picked up our bellowing charges in a mile-square piece of prairie called Section 34 and pushed them "slaunchwise," as Spike called it, across Section 27, north across Otter Creek, and on through Sections 15, 16, 17 and 18. While shafts of sunlight burst through the clouds, our unruly procession passed at a stately pace through an endlessly shifting backdrop of wild crags, canyons, buttes and tender meadows adrift in wild flowers. As our noisy charges trampled acres of timothy, broom, mustard, yellow sweet clover and sage they set off as many pungent vapors as the spice markets of Fez. Cows are obnoxious traveling companions, but it was a glorious trip.

The next day we chased them up the divide between Dry and Basin Creeks, through something called Wolf Park, down a rock slide which was so complicated I had to get off and lead Sleet so if she fell down it would be on me instead of the rocks, into Sweet Grass Canyon through a mill site, two sections that belong to the government, Eagle Park and the horse pasture of Section seven. The mill-site section already had stock grazing in it—brown and white Herefords, eager to confuse the genes of our Black Angus. "Kick 'em toward the box canyon," Spike yelled at us. "There is no use borrowing trouble." Unfortunately we borrowed quite a lot of trouble, in the form of

It all looks so calm, peaceful and reposed, but driving 200 Black Angus through the Crazies was anything but.

a large bull and several of his harem, but Spike was philosophical about it. As he said, "That's the romance of cowpunching."

Once we got the cows into their summer resort, we loaded eight 50-pound blocks of salt on two pack horses and spent a day distributing them in the highlands to make the grazing more tasty. The last day all we had to do was survive the nine-hour ride over a spectacular mountain divide ("If you don't like heights, look the other way," Barbie says), back into

Big Timber Canyon and the ranch. Barely in time for Sleet's day off.

Sleet was bored by the cows, bothered by the flies, impatient with the pace, and had a suppurating sore down near the girth that matched the ones I had covered with Band-Aids inside each kneecap. I figured her *real* problem was that she wasn't *paying* to be on the trip. "Only the rich," as one of the dudes said, as he happily tottered from the corral, "will pay to be miserable." (1967)

A mixture of sweetness and strength, Koerner's Madonna *portrayed the romantic ideal of western womanhood.*

The Whitney Gallery of Western Art houses the recreated Koerner studio above. Note the original Madonna.

About the Illustrations:

The vast majority of the art which appears throughout this book was done by past illustrators of *The Saturday Evening Post* and *The Country Gentleman.* Exceptions are a few color ads, courtesy of the General Motors Company and Texaco.

Black and white art by Philip Goodwin and others, and two-color pieces (the orange and black of the pre-1926 *Post*) by Harrison Fisher and Emlen Mc-Connell are among the illustrations. The full-color illustrations are by Benton Clark, Harvey Dunn, W.H.D. Koerner, Frederic Remington, Norman Rockwell, Mead Schaeffer, Frank E. Schoonover and several lesser-known artists. The most numerous are those of W.H.D. "Big Bill' Koerner.

Koerner was born in Germany in 1878 and came with his family to America at the age of two. This move was fortunate for us, as well as the Koerners, for it was to America, rather than to Germany, that this man gave of his great talent.

Early in his career, as art director of the *Chicago Tribune* and as a student of Howard Pyle, he applied his talent to varying subjects and techniques. But it wasn't until he illustrated Emerson Hough's *Traveling*

the Old Trails stories in 1919 that Koerner discovered the subject that would dominate his painting career—that of the American West.

"This is the first time in my career an artist has really pleased me with his work," Emerson Hough is quoted as saying upon seeing Koerner's *Madonna of the Prairie* in 1922 and it was again Emerson Hough, saying of yet another assignment, "We must have it right!" that prompted Koerner to take his family on an extensive tour of the West in 1924.

What the artist was able to sketch and absorb of the West at that time gave his subsequent works an authoritative authenticity which gained for him distinction among the most notable of painters of the American West—a distinction that has continued to be recognized and appreciated today, some 40 years after his death.

"He tells the truth in his pictures," his daughter, Ruth Koerner Oliver, says of her father's work. And it is with pride, and special thanks to her for her enthusiasm and cooperation in this project, that we present these poignant, yet powerful, works of W.H.D. Koerner, as well as those of his many distinguished colleagues.

Acknowledgments

Text Credits:

"Henry and the Golden Mine" by Stephen Vincent Benét, copyright 1939 by Stephen Vincent Benét, copyright © 1967 by Thomas C. Benét, Stephanie B. Mahin and Rachel Benét Lewis. Reprinted by permission of Brandt & Brandt Literary Agents, Inc.

"From the Big Woods to Plum Creek," an excerpt from "Let the Hurricane Roar" by Rose Wilder Lane. Reprinted by permission of Roger Lea MacBride.

"Hard Winter" by Oliver La Farge, copyright © 1933 by Oliver La Farge, copyright renewed © 1961 by Oliver La Farge. Reprinted by permission of the estate of the author.

Photo Credits:
Page: 7, W.H.D. Koerner (1878-1938); 16, Culver Pictures; 19, The Bettmann Archive; 22, General Motors Corporation; 32, The Bettmann Archive; 40, 41, Texaco; 43, W.H.D. Koerner (1878-1938); 44, Brown Brothers; 74 & 77, National Archives; 88, The Dow Chemical Company; 93, W.H.D. Koerner (1878-1938); 98, 106, Oklahoma Historical Society.

Illustrations and text not otherwise credited are from the pages of The *Saturday Evening Post* or *The Country Gentleman* and are the copyrighted property of The Curtis Publishing Company or The Saturday Evening Post Company.